Refusing to Be a Man

John Stoltenberg

REFUSING
TO BE A MAN

Essays on Sex and Justice

Breitenbush Books Inc. : Portland, Oregon

Library of Congress Cataloging-in-Publication Data:

Stoltenberg, John.
  Refusing to be a man : essays on sex and justice / John Stoltenberg.
  ISBN 0-932576-73-7 : $16.95
  1. Men—United States—Sexual behavior. 2. Masculinity (Psychology) 3. Sex role—
United States. 4. Machismo—United States. 5. Sexism—United States. 6. Women—United
States—Crimes against.   I. Title.
HQ28.S86 1989
306.7'088041—dc 19   89-607

Breitenbush Books, Inc., P.O. Box 82157, Portland, Oregon 97282
James Anderson, Publisher
Patrick Ames, Editor-in-Chief

Breitenbush Books are distributed by Taylor Publishing Co., Dallas, Texas

Text design by Ky Krauthamer
Title page art by Casey P. Tabb
Manufactured in the United States of America

For Andrea

In memory of Jimmy

Contents

Preface   1

Part I: The Ethics of Male Sexual Identity

Rapist Ethics   9
How Men Have (a) Sex   25
Sexual Objectification and Male Supremacy   41

Part II: The Politics of Male Sexual Identity

Eroticism and Violence in the Father-Son Relationship   59
Disarmament and Masculinity   77

The Fetus as Penis: Men's Self-interest and Abortion Rights   91
What Is "Good Sex"?   101

Part III: Pornography and Male Supremacy

The Forbidden Language of Sex   117
Pornography and Freedom   123
Confronting Pornography as a Civil-Rights Issue   137

Part IV: Activism and Moral Selfhood

Feminist Activism and Male Sexual Identity   175
Other Men   187
Battery and the Will to Freedom   199

About the Essays   205
Notes   211

The world's definitions are one thing and the life one actually lives is quite another. One cannot allow oneself, nor can one's family, friends, or lovers—to say nothing of one's children—to live according to the world's definitions: one must find a way, perpetually, to be stronger and better than that.

James Baldwin

Preface

When the ideas of feminism first reached me about fifteen years ago, almost every detail of my life began to change, in ways I still don't fully comprehend. Since then I've been asked, probably hundreds of times, "What got you so interested in feminism anyway?" The question, or a version of it, is usually asked with bewilderment, though sometimes with frank suspicion—as if growing up a man and becoming a feminist (a radical one, at that) were off the map of human possibility.

I try to explain, as best I can, that beginning in 1974 I happened to be really challenged by some close women friends and some mind-blowing feminist books and hours and hours of intense discussion—all of which is true as far as it goes. But like so many men I've met across the country through profeminist activism over the past decade and a half, I count myself part of the struggle for women's equality for reasons that are intensely personal—so personal, sometimes, they can't be glibly declared.

I'm thinking of those men whose feminist convictions spring from loyalty to a particular woman in their lives—a mother, a lover, a cherished friend—someone who has brought them to an intimate, almost insider's view of what life for women is like under male supremacy. These men have made a vow to stand beside her and not abandon her, to wholeheartedly be her ally. For such men, loyalty to a woman's life is experienced as a profound form of intimacy (not a threat to selfhood, as it might be for other men).

I'm thinking also of those men whose commitment to feminism draws on their own experience of sexual violence or sexual abuse from other men, perhaps as a child or adolescent. Somehow such men have not paved over what happened to them; rather, they have recognized in it the same dimensions of violence and abuse that *women* were mobilizing to resist. So these men, for their own silent reasons, have cast their lot with the feminist struggle for freedom and bodily integrity—because they know full well it's what *everyone* should have.

I'm thinking also of those men who have become feminists in part because they have suffered the shame of growing up with a sexuality that was not "standard issue." It was a sexuality that longed for partnership and ardent tenderness; it did not stir at dominance and coercion. It was a sexuality that set them apart, whether with women or other men. These men have become, in a sense, dissidents from the sex-class hierarchy in intimacy; and they are gathering courage to defy that hierarchy beyond the bedroom as well.

I'm thinking also of those men whose advocacy of feminism derives from other sorts of principled political activism. Coming from the perspective of their pacifism, their antiracism, or their commitment to economic justice, for instance, these men have grasped the ideals of radical feminism with a seriousness and intellectual honesty such that they now regard feminism as logically consistent with—no, *integral to*—any human-rights struggle worthy of the name. Cerebral though it may seem at times, their commitment, in its own way, is also from the heart.

What would happen if we each told the deepest truth about why we are men who mean to be part of the feminist revolution—why we can't *not* be part of it—why its vision of full humanity for everyone so moves us? What would happen if we dared? As the poet Muriel Rukeyser once asked, I wonder sometimes: would the world split open?

I wrote this book without exactly knowing I was writing a book. All but one of these essays were originally written to be spoken aloud to specific audiences, written to be spoken face-to-face, to someone I hoped would understand.* For over a decade before I began writing these speeches, I was a playwright, writing for the voices of impersonators while I stood aside, as if prompting from the wings, feeding imagined characters made-up lines. But when my life was changed by radical feminism, I began to write what my own voice needed to say. I felt an urgency to write words that I could stand behind with conviction, words that I could trust to say out loud in public because I had thrashed them out in private until they were as true as I could get them, until they said exactly what I meant, exactly what I believed, even if those words might provoke some people to outrage.

I almost never knew where an essay would lead when I began it. Usually, I began with a question, or a set of questions, or a seemingly intractable fact of my life that resisted my understanding, or a sense of a philosophical dilemma that taunted me to inquire into it. Then I would work at it through writing, sometimes for as long as a year, until I had figured something out, something that would have clear meaning beyond my personal brain. In that sense these essays are implicitly

---

* See "About the Essays," pp. 205–209.

autobiographical, even though not made up of personal disclosures. And in that sense *Refusing to Be a Man* refers as much to what this book is about as to how it came to be written.

Several of the speeches were emotionally momentous when I first spoke them. For instance, I wrote "The Fetus as Penis: Men's Self-interest and Abortion Rights" and ventured from New York City out to Los Angeles to deliver it to over five hundred people at a national antisexist men's conference. I imagined beforehand they would hate what it said—I was, after all, calling for the end of manhood as we know it—and I rather expected to be booed off the stage. On the contrary, to my astonishment, they greeted the speech with an almost-all-standing ovation—the first time it occurred to me there might really be some numbers of men out there who wouldn't turn on someone who wanted the whole male-supremacist setup destroyed.

Taken together, these essays expose and challenge what goes on in men's minds and bodies and lives in order to maintain their belief that they are "men." Coursing through this book is my analysis that "the male sex" requires injustice in order to exist. Male sexual identity is entirely a political and ethical construction, I argue; and masculinity has personal meaning only because certain acts, choices, and policies create it—with devastating consequences for human society. But precisely *because* that personal and social identity is constructed, we can refuse it, we can act against it—we can change. The core of our being can choose allegiance to justice instead.

This book is about the interrelationship of sexual politics and sexual ethics, and the possibility of an emerging selfhood rooted in one's capacity for fairness (rather than in one's ongoing crisis of sexual identity). Though intended as a theory of liberation, this book is, in some respects, much better than my life. I know I have not always lived up to the values it recommends. But I believe that I have been honest in divulging the meaning of what I know, based on the life I have lived and the lives I have witnessed. And I believe there are others who will recognize the possibility of authentic liberation that this book points to.

If male sexual identity is a social and political construction that is inextricably linked to male supremacy, as this book argues, then what does it mean to "refuse to be a man"? Male sexual identity exists, in part, because people born with penises learn an ethic of sexual injustice, an ethic that leaves out specific others. In order to distinguish themselves as real "men," they learn not to know what can be known about the values in what they do to others, specifically anyone who is "less a man." So to begin with, refusing to be a man means learning a radical new ethic: determining to learn as much as one can know about the values in the acts one has done and the acts one chooses to do and their full consequences for other people—as if everyone else is absolutely as real as oneself.

This book is for people who—like me—have wanted such an ethic of sexual justice in the world, far more than we knew.

John Stoltenberg

New York City
November 1988

Part I

The Ethics of Male Sexual Identity

Rapist Ethics

Stories have beginnings, middles, and endings. Ideas do not. Stories can be told and understood in terms of who did what and what happened to whom, what happened next, and what happened after that. Ideas do not exist in time and space that way, yet it is only through our apprehension of certain ideas that historical reality makes any sense at all. We interpret all the data of our senses—including characters, actions, consequences, even our so-called selves—according to ideas, concepts, or mental structures, some of which we understand, some of which we just believe.

Sexual identity is an idea. Sexual identity—the belief that there is maleness and femaleness and that one is either male or female—is among the most fundamental ideas with which we interpret our experience. Not only do we "know" and "believe in" the idea of sexual identity, but the idea of sexual identity largely determines how and what we know. With the idea of sexual identity in our head, we see things and feel things and learn things in terms of it. Like a sketch artist who looks at a still life or figure and sees lines to be drawn where in fact there are contours and surfaces that wrap around out of sight, we observe human beings about us and distinguish appearances and behaviors belonging to a male sexual identity or a female sexual identity. We say to ourselves, "There goes a man," "There goes a woman." Like the sketch artist, we draw lines at the edges beyond which we cannot see.

The idea of sexual identity, in fact, has a claim on us that our actual experience does not; for if our experience "contradicts" it, we will bend our experience so that it will make sense in terms of the idea. Other ideas—such as our belief that there is an up and a down and that objects will tend to fall toward earth—are supportable with much less mental effort. Gravity is a sturdy, reliable category into which most of our everyday experience fits without much fiddling. No one need worry their head that gravity will somehow cease if too many people abandon faith in it. Nor need we contend with the occasional exceptions that could nag us and cause us anxiety about whether, say, a dropped object will truly fall. The force of gravity would be with us even without our idea of it. Gravity just is; we don't have to make it be. Not so the idea of sexual identity. Sexual identity is a political idea. Its force derives entirely from the human effort required to sustain it, and it requires the lifelong, nearly full-time exertion of everybody for its maintenance and verification. Though everyone, to some extent, plays their part in keeping the idea of sexual identity real, some people, it should be noted, work at this project with more fervor than do others.

We are remarkably resistant to recognizing the idea of sexual identity as having solely a political meaning. We very much prefer to believe, instead, that it has a metaphysical existence. For instance, we want to think that the idea of sexual identity "exists" the way that the idea of a chair does. The idea of a chair can have an actual existence in the form of a real chair. There can be many different kinds of chairs, but we can know one when we see one, because we have the idea of a chair in our head. And every actual chair has a degree of permanence to its chairness; we can look at it and sit in it today and tomorrow and the day after that and know it solidly as a chair. We believe the idea of sexual identity can have such a continuity and permanence too, in the form of a real man or a real woman. We believe that though people's appearances and behaviors differ greatly, we can know a real man or a real woman when we see one, because we have the ideas of maleness and femaleness in our head. We think that when we perceive this maleness or femaleness in another person, that person's sexual identity has a durability, a constancy, a certainty—to themselves as well as to us. We think that it is truly possible for us ourselves to be a real man or a real woman with the same certainty that we see in others. We think the idea of sexual identity is an idea like the idea of a chair, yet we can be dimly aware at moments that the idea of one's sexual identity is sometimes in doubt, is never fully realized, never settled, never really "there" for any dependable length of time. We can observe that, oddly, the idea of one's own sexual identity must be re-created, over and over again, in action and sensation—in doing things that make one feel really male or really female and in not doing things that leave room for doubt. To each person's own self, the idea of a fixed and certain sexual identity can seem "out there" somewhere, elusive, always more fully realized in someone else. Almost everyone thinks someone else's sexual identity is more real than one's own, and almost everyone measures themselves against other people who are perceived to be more male or more female. At the same time, almost everyone's own sexual identity feels certain and real to themselves only fleetingly, with troublesome interruptions. Chairs do not seem to have the same problem, and we do not have the same problem with chairs.

Many attempts have been made to locate a basis in material reality for our belief in sexual identity. For instance, it is claimed quite scientifically that people think and behave as they do, in a male way or in a female way, because of certain molecules called hormones, which with rather circular logic are designated male or female. It is said, quite scientifically, that the prenatal presence or absence of these hormones produces male brains or female brains—brains predisposed to think gender-typed thoughts and to act out gender-typed behaviors. In fetuses becoming male, it is said, allegedly male hormones called androgens "masculinize" the brain cells by, among other things, chemically connecting the brain-wave pathways for sex and aggression, so that eroticism and terrorism will ever after be mental neighbors. It is also said that in fetuses becoming female those androgens are absent, so those two circuits do not fuse. The scientists who study and document such phenomena (most of whom, of course, believe their brains to be quite male) claim to have determined that some female fetuses receive an abnormal overdose of androgens in the womb, an accident that explains, they say, why tomboy girls climb trees and why uppity women want careers. The gist of such theories—and there are many others that are similar—is that behavior follows sexual identity, rather than the other way around.

If it is true that behavior follows sexual identity, then the rightness or wrongness of any human action can justifiably be judged differently depending on whether it was done by a male or a female, on grounds such as biology, the natural order, or human nature. The cross-cultural indisposition of able-bodied males to do dishes, to pick up after themselves, or to handle child-care responsibilities, for example, can be said to derive from their hormonal constitutions, which were engineered for stalking mastodons and which have not evolved for doing the laundry.

Nearly all people believe deeply and unshakably that some things are wrong for a woman to do while right for a man and that other things are wrong for a man to do while right for a woman. This faith, like most, is blind; but unlike most, it does not perceive itself as a faith. It is, in fact, an ethic without an epistemology—a particular system of attaching values to conduct without the slightest comprehension of how or why people believe that the system is true. It is a creed whose articles never really require articulation, because its believers rarely encounter anyone who does not already believe it, silently and by heart. The valuation of human actions according to the gender of the one who acts is a notion so unremarkable, so unremittingly commonplace, and so self-evident to so many that its having come under any scrutiny whatsoever is a major miracle in the history of human consciousness.

Oddly, at the same time, many people cherish a delusion that their ethical judgments are really gender-neutral. In popular psychobabble, for instance, one hears the words "give and take" in countless conversations about interpersonal relationships between men and women. The catchphrase evokes both the ideal and the practical possibility of a perfectly reciprocal dyadic relationship, in harmony and equilibrium, exchanging back and forth, like a blissfully unbiased teeter-totter. Men and women alike will swear by it, extolling giving and taking as if it were a first principle of socio-sexual interaction. The actual reality beneath "give and take" may be quite different: for her, swallowed pride and self-effacing forgiveness; from him, punishing emotional withdrawal and egomaniacal defensiveness. Or perhaps they will trade off tears for temporary reforms, capitulation for a moment's tranquillity, her subordination in exchange for an end to his threats of force. They will speak of this drama, embittering and brutalizing, as "give and take," the only form they can imagine for a love across the chasm that keeps male distinct from female. They may grieve over their failed communication, yet they will defend to the teeth their tacit sex-specific ethics—by which men and women are held accountable to two different systems of valuing conduct—and they will not, ever, comprehend what has gone wrong.

In no arena of human activity are people more loyal to that sex-specific ethics than in transactions involving overt genital stimulation. When people have sex, make love, or screw, they act as a rule in conformity with two separate systems of behavior valuation, one male and one female, as if their identities or lives depended on it. For males, generally, it tends to be their identities; for females, often, it is more a matter of their lives. Behaving within the ethical limits of what is wrong or right for their sexual identities becomes so critical, in fact, that physicalized anxiety about whether one is "male enough" or "female enough" is virtually indistinguishable from most bodily sensations that are regarded as "erotic." For a male, the boundaries of what he wants to make happen in a sexual encounter with a partner—when and for how long, and to whom he wants it to happen—are rarely unrelated to this pivotal consideration: what is necessary in order "to be the man there," in order to experience the functioning of his own body "as a male," and in order to be regarded by his partner as having no tactile, visual, behavioral, or emotional resemblance to a *not*-male, a female. The anxiety he feels— fearing he may not be able to make that happen and striving to inhabit his body so that it *will* happen—is a component of the sexual tension he feels. For many females, deference to a male partner's overriding identity anxiety can know no bounds; for her, the fear is that his precariously rigged sexual-arousal mechanism will go awry, haywire, and that he will hold her responsible and punish her somehow for turning him off (Or is it for turning him on to begin with? That part is never clear). To avoid that fate, that can of hysterical worms, no sacrifice no matter how demeaning can be too great. In such ways as these are most people's experiences of sexual tension due in large measure to their anxiety about whether they are behaving within the ethical parameters of what is wrong or right conduct for their putative sexual identities. The sexual tension and the gender anxiety are so closely associated within everyone's body and brain that the anxiety predictably triggers the tension and the release of the tension can be expected to absolve the anxiety—at least until next time.

This, then, is the nexus of eroticism and ethics—the hookup between the eroticism we feel and the ethics of our acts, between sensation and action, between feeling and doing. It is a connection at the core of both our selves and our culture. It is the point at which gender-specific sexuality emerges from behavioral choices, not from anatomy. It is the point at which our erotic feelings make manifest the fear with which we conform to the structure of right and wrong for either gender, a structure mined on all sides by every peril we dare imagine. This is the point at which we might recognize that our very sexual identities are artifices and illusions, the result of a lifetime of striving to do the right male thing not the right female thing, or the right female thing not the right male thing. This is the point, too, at which we can see that we are not dealing with anything so superficial as roles, images, or stereotypes, but that in fact we have come face to face with an aspect of our identities even more basic than our corporeality—namely, our faith that there are two sexes and our secret and public desperation to belong to one not the other.

The fiction of a sexual identity becomes clearer upon examining more closely the case of male sexual identity. What exactly is the set of behaviors that are prescribed as right for it and proscribed as wrong? How does someone learn to know the difference? What is the difference between the male right and wrong and the female right and wrong? And how is it possible that someone who has successfully attained a male sexual identity can feel so right in doing an action—for instance, rape—that to someone else, someone female, is so totally wrong?

That last question reduces, approximately, to Why do men rape? As a preliminary answer, I propose an analogy to the craft of acting in the theater:

There is a theory of acting, quite common today, that to achieve recognizable naturalism, an actor must play a character as if everything that character does is completely justifiable; so, for instance, an actor playing a villain ought not "play" villainousness, or the evilness of that character. Only an untrained or amateur actor would ever try to portray the quality of maliciousness in a character who does morally decrepit things (the roles of Shakespeare's Richard the Third and Büchner's Woyzeck come to mind). Rather, according to this theory, the actor must believe at all times that what the character is doing is right, no matter what the audience or the other characters onstage may think of the goodness or badness of that character's actions. The actor playing the part must pursue the character's objectives in each scene, wholly believing that there is absolutely nothing wrong with doing so. Although in the eyes of observers the character might commit the most heinous crimes, the actor playing the character must have prepared for the role by adopting a belief system in which it makes moral sense to do those acts.

The problem of portraying character in the theater is one that Aristotle dissected in his classic fifth century B.C. text *Poetics*. His points are still central to acting theory as it is practiced today:

With regard to . . . characters, there are four things to be aimed at. First, and most important, they must be good. Now any speech or action that manifests some kind of moral purpose will be expressive of character: the character will be good if the purpose is good. The goodness is possible in every class of persons. Even a woman may be good, and also a slave, though the one is liable to be an inferior being, and the other quite worthless. The second thing to aim at is appropriateness. There is a type of manly valor, but manliness in a woman, or unscrupulous cleverness, is inappropriate. Thirdly, a character must be true to life: which is something quite different from goodness and appropriateness, as here described. The fourth point is consistency: for even though the person being imitated . . . is inconsistent, still he must be consistently inconsistent.[1]

The impersonation of male sexual identity in life bears several striking resemblances to the techniques by which an actor portrays character. Paraphrasing Aristotle's admonitions from twenty-five centuries ago, one can generalize that to act out convincingly a male sexual identity requires:

• an unfailing belief in one's own goodness and the moral rightness of one's purposes, regardless of how others may value what one does;
• a rigorous adherence to the set of behaviors, characteristics, and idiosyncrasies that are appropriately male (and therefore inappropriate for a female);

• an unquestioning belief in one's own consistency, notwithstanding any evidence to the contrary—a consistency rooted, for all practical purposes, in the relentlessness of one's will and in the fact that, being superior by social definition, one can want whatever one wants and one can expect to get it.

This much, we can assume, Aristotle meant by "true to life," for in fact in life this is how male sexual identity is acted out, and this is how "maleness" is inferred and assessed—as, fundamentally, a characterological phenomenon. Most people, whether as spectators of real life or staged life, regard as credible and laudable someone's convictions about the rightness of what that one is doing—no matter what, at no matter what cost—when that someone is a male, operating within the behavioral choices of male sexual identity. A "he," being a he, can get away with murder—figuratively, and sometimes even literally—simply by virtue of the fact that he dissembles so sincerely, or he uses up someone's life with such single-minded purpose, or he betrays someone's trust with such resolute passion, or he abandons commitments with such panache. When men are held to account for what they do in their lives to women— which happens relatively rarely—their tunnel vision, their obliviousness to consequences, their egotism, their willfulness, all tend to excuse, rather than compound, their most horrific interpersonal offenses. Someone female, however, is regarded very differently. What is expected of her is hesitancy, qualms, uncertainty that what she is doing is right—even while doing something right. She should, as Aristotle might have put it, play her part as if in perpetual stage fright, a comely quality befitting one as inferior as she. And when she is called to account—which happens relatively often—not only is there never an excuse, but her lack of appropriate faintheartedness may be grounds for yet more blame.

Blame, of course, figures prominently in what happens when a man rapes a woman: The man commits the rape, then the woman gets blamed for it. If rape was a transaction where gender-specific ethics were not operative, that assessment of responsibility would be regarded as the *non sequitur* it is. But in rape that illogic is believed to explain what happened and why: If a man rapes a woman, the woman is responsible; therefore the rape is not a rape. What is the meaning of that nonsensical blaming? And how does it illuminate the structure of sex-specific ethics?

According to the tacit ethics of male sexual identity, one who would act out the character of "a man, not a woman" will necessarily believe that the series of actions appropriate to that character is right and that there is absolutely nothing wrong with doing anything in pursuit of the character's objectives. Rape is, of course, such an action in that it is committed almost exclusively by those who are acting out the character of "a man, not a woman." Rape is not the only action that is congruent with the tacit ethics of male sexual identity. Wife beating, for instance, is another. So, for that matter, are any number of things men do every day that are faithless, heedless, irresponsible, or humiliating in relation to women—things men do with impunity and women suffer silently because "that's just how men are." If ever a woman decides not to suffer such an offense silently—if, for instance, she decides not to tolerate being treated as if she is less of person than he—and if she decides to confront him on terms that come close to exposing the gender-specific ethics in what he has done ("You acted just like a man. You treated me as if I completely didn't matter just because I'm a woman"), she will likely experience his vengeful defensiveness at gale force; and he will likely try to blow her away. That sorry scenario is also consistent with the tacit ethics by which male sexual identity is played out. Sex-specific ethics are tacit and they must remain tacit, otherwise the jig would be up.[2]

The series of actions that are appropriate to the character of "a man, not a woman" is profoundly influenced by the presence of rape among them. This series of acts is not like a dissonance composed of random, unharmonious notes. It is, rather, a chord in which the root or fundament colors every pitch above it, its overtones enhancing every note that is struck. Rape is like the fundamental tone; played sometimes fortissimo, sometimes pianissimo, sometimes a mere echo, it determines the harmonics of the whole chord. "Sometimes," "just a little," "now and then," "only rarely"—however much one may wish to qualify the salient feature of the series, the act of prevailing upon another to admit of penetration without full and knowledgeable assent so sets the standard in the repertoire of male-defining behaviors that it is not at all inaccurate to suggest that the ethics of male sexual identity are essentially rapist.

Rapist ethics is a definitive and internally consistent system for attaching value to conduct: The concepts of both right and wrong exist within rapist ethics; it is not an ethic in which blame and moral condemnation go unreckoned or unremarked. There is also in rapist ethics a structural view of personal responsibility for acts, but it views the one *to whom* the act is done as being responsible for the act. It is a little like the driver of a car believing 'hat the tree beside the road caused the car to collide with it. For example, one victim of a rape told an interviewer:

There he was, a man who had the physical power to lock me up and rape me, without any real threat of societal punishment, telling *me* that *I* was oppressive because I was a woman! Then he started telling me he could understand how men sometimes go out and rape women. . . . He looked at me and said, "Don't make me hurt you," as though I was, by not giving in to him, forcing him to rape me. That's how he justified the whole thing. He kept saying women were forcing him to rape them by not being there when he needed them.[3]

This reversal of moral accountability is not an isolated instance; it is a characteristic of nearly all acts that are committed within the ethic of male sexual identity. It is a type of projection, of seeing one's "wrong" in the person one is wronging, which is the same as saying that one has done no wrong. Social scientists who have surveyed the attitudes of prisoners report that "[s]ex offenders are twice as likely to insist on their own innocence as the general offenders" and that "they frequently see in their victims aggressive, offensive persons who force them into abnormal acts." [4]

And a psychiatrist who has worked extensively with admitted rapists reports, "It is becoming increasingly more difficult for these men to see their actions as criminal, as being anything more than the normal male response to a female." [5]

In the twisted logic of rapist ethics, the victim is ultimately culpable; the victim is the culprit; the victim did the wrong. Absurdly, the most obvious and absolute facts about the act—who did what to whom—become totally obfuscated because responsibility is imputed to the victim for an act that someone else committed. Myths that promulgate this ethic abound: Women want to be raped, women deserve to be raped, women provoke rape, women need to be raped, and women *enjoy* being raped. The societal force of these myths is so great that many rape victims fear to reveal to anyone what has happened to them, believing themselves to be the cause of what happened. Several years after she was gang-raped at the age of fourteen, for instance, a woman recalled:

I felt like I'd brought out the worst in these men just by being an available female body on the road. I felt like if I hadn't been on the road, these men would have continued in their good upstanding ways, and that it was my fault that they'd been lowered to rape me. [6]

Also, she remembered:

I forgave them immediately. I felt like it was all my fault that I'd been raped. I said, well, they're men. They just can't help themselves. That's the way men are. [7]

Implicit in this victim's recollected feelings are the twin tenets of rapist ethics: It is right to rape; it is wrong to be raped. That translates more often than not into a precept even more appalling yet probably closer to the raw insides of male-supremacist eroticism: It is right to be male; it is wrong to be female. Or, in the words of a character who has just raped, beaten, and forcibly sodomized his wife in the pornographic novel *Juliette* by the Marquis de Sade:

There are two sides to every passion . . . : seen from the side of the victim upon whom the pressure is brought to bear, the passion appears unjust; whereas . . . to him who applies the pressure, his passion is the justest thing imaginable.[8]

It is right to be male; it is wrong to be female; therefore anything done against a woman to the purpose of one's passion—realizing male sexual identity—is justifiable and good within the frame of rapist ethics.

In rape, in addition to the physical act, a transaction occurs that can be understood as the obliteration of the victim's moral identity. In an act of rape, the ethical structure of male right and wrong jams or destroys the victim's sense of herself as someone who is responsible for her own acts; rapist ethics disintegrates her accumulated knowledge of acts and consequences and of the relation between herself and her own acts. She regards herself as "at fault" for the assault, perhaps "forgiving" of her assailant at the same time, taking upon herself all the blame there is to be had, because the most basic connection has been severed—the connection between her identity and her own real deeds. The obliteration can result in a near total eclipse of her sense of herself as a being with integrity, as ever actually having had the capacity for moral deciding, rational thought, and conscientious action. The one who rapes, on the other hand, experiences himself as reintegrated, miraculously made whole again, more vital and more real. Rapists often report that they felt "bad" before they raped—and that's why they set out to rape—but that they felt "better" afterward, that the rape itself was stimulating, exciting, enjoyable, and fun. The disintegration of the victim's sense of self is, one might say, a prerequisite for the integration of the rapist's sense of self—a dynamic that is replicated whenever anyone acts within the ethical structure of male sexual identity. As one man said, succinctly stating the modern and ancient male dilemma: "A man gotta have a woman or he don't know he's a man." [9]

Some actions congruent with rapist ethics are committed with what appears to be a "conscience" that is not quite clear. It would seem that while committing the act with complete conviction, the actor who does it experiences some remorse as well. This familiar show of contrition is apparent in the following, a story told by a woman about her twenty-four-year-old husband:

He didn't only hit me. He bit me and tore my hair. I have a scar on my arm from where he bit a hole out of it one time. The only way to end the beating situation was to become submissive, so it could go on for hours and hours and hours until I couldn't take it any longer, and I'd end up on the floor a sobbing heap, and then he would continue kicking at me for a while. Then he would pick me up and brush the tears away and tell me how sorry he was. And he'd ask me to stay in so that people wouldn't see the black eye and bruises. Another trip he laid on me was how heavy it was for him to deal with his guilt about beating me. [10]

On the face of the matter, remorse, regret, or guilt would seem to contradict the unequivocal conviction with which a man acts out rapist ethics, since all responsibility for "wrongdoing" has been imputed to the victim, the female, the one to whom the act was done. Perplexingly, there does sometimes occur a kind of ritual dance of repentance after certain acts, especially brutal ones, through which men realize male sexual identity. It is as if one can hear the man murmuring some lyrical longing for atonement and propitiation: "I'm sorry, forgive me, I didn't mean to, I apologize; I promise I will never do it again." The refrain about refraining.

What is the erotic substructure of that swift transition from violence and brutality to pangs of remorse? How are we to understand what happens once a man has teased (perhaps) or toyed with, or betrayed or humiliated, or attacked or terrorized a woman and then he turns suddenly repentant, and just as suddenly he indicates that what he wants to do now is fuck her? And what are we to make of his entreaties for forgiveness, for another chance, for reconciliation? his protestations of self-reproach? the woebegone look in his eyes? Is there, after all, such a thing in rapist ethics as a genuine moral consciousness of the true consequences of one's acts to other actual human beings?

The answer, I think, is no.

I believe that for those who strive toward male sexual identity, there is always the critical problem of how to manage one's affairs so that one always has available a supply of sustenance in the form of feminine deference and submission—someone female to whom to do the things that will adequately realize one's maleness. The sustenance must be personal, from one or more particular females who are in personal relation to oneself. The appeal for "forgiveness" within any such relationship functions to trap and lock in any female who may have been considering withdrawing her sustenance from him. The forgiveness asked—though it is almost always demanded, because even here pressure is applied—is a form of insistence that she remain in relation to him. One who lives by rapist ethics, after all, constantly risks alienating the objects of his pressures and passions—and with good reason. But forgiveness elicited at those critical moments seduces the woman back into victimization. Without that relation, male sexual identity withers. As one man put it: "When women are losing their will to be women ... how can men be men? What the hell have we got to be male about any more?" [11] The unforgiving woman is the judging woman, the angry woman, the withdrawing woman; she has lost her will to be a woman as men define it. Forgiveness from a woman represents her continued commitment to be present for him, to stay in relationship to him, enabling him to remain by contrast male. Her charity, her mercy, her grace (not for nothing have men personified all those abstractions as female in legend and art!) are in fact the emblems of female subordination to rapist ethics.

Now I have delineated the structure of a particular ethic, the ethics of male sexual identity—its value system, its dynamics, its basic scenarios, the way it functions to create male sexual identity out of the ashes of female selflessness. It is the value system in which some acts are deemed "good" and "right" because they serve to make an individual's idea of maleness real, and others "bad" or "wrong" because they numb it. Having read this far, one may well ask: What is the use? "What is the use?" meaning: It all seems so hopeless. And "What is the use?" meaning: What is the practical value?—what good does it do to know that eroticism, ethics, and gender identity are fundamentally interrelated?

If we do not understand that interrelatedness, then indeed there is no hope. But there is enormous promise in perceiving gender as an ethically constructed phenomenon—a belief we create by how we decide to act, not something that we automatically "are" on account of how we are born. To be sure, for there to be any real hope of change, it means that men must examine scrupulously and honestly how we actually behave, the real facts about our acts and our responsibilities, what happens to whom as a result, and men must own the consequences of what we have done. Men will have to stop the rapist-ethics mindfuck—imputing "oppressiveness" to anyone who refuses to give in, ignoring the word "no," disregarding completely the reality of anyone who is not fawning and flattering and full of awe for our masculine prerogative. And men will no longer be entitled to defend our choices—and they *are* choices— by appeal to those dear substances our brain cells, our hormones, our gonads, our DNA. And yes, the idea of giving up our deep attachment rapist ethics is frightening at first. But I believe that when men do begin to look at how we act the way we do in order to re-create certainty about our otherwise elusive gender—and how our gender identity is the result, not the cause, of the rape-like values in our conduct—then we may begin to grasp that it is thoroughly possible to *change* how we act.

For there to be hope, nothing matters more.

24

How Men Have (a) Sex

An address to college students

In the human species, how many sexes are there?
Answer A: *There are two sexes.*
Answer B: *There are three sexes.*
Answer C: *There are four sexes.*
Answer D: *There are seven sexes.*
Answer E: *There are as many sexes as there are people.*

I'd like to take you, in an imaginary way, to look at a different world, somewhere else in the universe, a place inhabited by a life form that very much resembles us. But these creatures grow up with a peculiar knowledge. They know that they have been born in an infinite variety. They know, for instance, that in their genetic material they are born with hundreds of different chromosome formations at the point in each cell that we would say determines their "sex." These creatures don't just come in XX or XY; they also come in XXY and XYY and XXX plus a long list of "mosaic" variations in which some cells in a creature's body have one combination and other cells have another. Some of these creatures are born with chromosomes that aren't even quite X or Y because a little bit of one chromosome goes and gets joined to another. There are hundreds of different combinations, and though all are not fertile, quite a number of them are. The creatures in this world enjoy their individuality; they delight in the fact that they are not divisible into distinct categories. So when another newborn arrives with an esoterically rare chromosomal formation, there is a little celebration: "Aha," they say, "another sign that we are each unique."

These creatures also live with the knowledge that they are born with a vast range of genital formations. Between their legs are tissue structures that vary along a continuum, from clitorises with a vulva through all possible combinations and gradations to penises with a scrotal sac. These creatures live with an understanding that their genitals all developed prenatally from exactly the same little nub of embryonic tissue called a genital tubercle, which grew and developed under the influence of varying amounts of the hormone androgen. These creatures honor and respect everyone's natural-born genitalia—including what we would describe as a microphallus or a clitoris several inches long. What these creatures find amazing and precious is that because everyone's genitals stem from the same embryonic tissue, the nerves inside all their genitals got wired very much alike, so these nerves of touch just go crazy upon contact in a way that resonates completely between them. "My gosh," they think, "you must feel something in your genital tubercle that intensely resembles what I'm feeling in my genital tubercle." Well, they don't exactly *think* that in so many words; they're actually quite heavy into their feelings at that point; but they do feel very connected—throughout all their wondrous variety.

I could go on. I could tell you about the variety of hormones that course through their bodies in countless different patterns and proportions, both before birth and throughout their lives—the hormones that we call "sex hormones" but that they call "individuality inducers." I could tell you how these creatures think about reproduction: For part of their lives, some of them are quite capable of gestation, delivery, and lactation; and for part of their lives, some of them are quite capable of insemination; and for part or all of their lives, some of them are not capable of any of those things—so these creatures conclude that it would be silly to lock anyone into a lifelong category based on a capability variable that may or may not be utilized and that in any case changes over each lifetime in a fairly uncertain and idiosyncratic way. These creatures are not oblivious to reproduction; but nor do they spend their lives constructing a self-definition around their variable reproductive capacities. They don't have to, because what is truly unique about these creatures is that they are capable of having a sense of personal identity without struggling to fit into a group identity based on how they were born. These creatures are quite happy, actually. They don't worry about sorting *other* creatures into categories, so they don't have to worry about whether they are measuring up to some category they themselves are supposed to belong to.

These creatures, of course, have sex. Rolling and rollicking and robust sex, and sweaty and slippery and sticky sex, and trembling and quaking and tumultuous sex, and tender and tingling and transcendent sex. They have sex fingers to fingers. They have sex belly to belly. They have sex genital tubercle to genital tubercle. They *have* sex. They do not have *a* sex. In their erotic lives, they are not required to act out their status in a category system—because there *is* no category system. There are no sexes to belong to, so sex between creatures is free to be between genuine individuals—not representatives of a category. They have sex. They do not have a sex. Imagine life like that.

Perhaps you have guessed the point of this science fiction: Anatomically, each creature in the imaginary world I have been describing could be an identical twin of every human being on earth. These creatures, in fact, *are us*—in every way except socially and politically. The way they are born is the way we are born. And we are not born belonging to one or the other of two sexes. We are born into a physiological continuum on which there is no discrete and definite point that you can call "male" and no discrete and definite point that you can call "female." If you look at all the variables in nature that are said to determine human "sex," you can't possibly find one that will unequivocally split the species into two. Each of the so-called criteria of sexedness is itself a continuum—including chromosomal variables, genital and gonadal variations, reproductive capacities, endocrinological proportions, and any other criterion you could think of. Any or all of these different variables may line up in any number of ways, and all of the variables may vary independently of one another.[1]

What does all this mean? It means, first of all, a logical dilemma: Either human "male" and human "female" actually exist in nature as fixed and discrete entities and you can credibly base an entire social and political system on those absolute natural categories, or else the variety of human sexedness is infinite. As Andrea Dworkin wrote in 1974:

The discovery is, of course, that "man" and "woman" are fictions, caricatures, cultural constructs. As models they are reductive, totalitarian, inappropriate to human becoming. As roles they are static, demeaning to the female, dead-ended for male and female both.[2]

The conclusion is inescapable:

We are, clearly, a multisexed species which has its sexuality spread along a vast continuum where the elements called male and female are not discrete.[3]

"*We are . . . a multisexed species.*" I first read those words a little over ten years ago—and that liberating recognition saved my life.

All the time I was growing up, I knew that there was something really problematical in my relationship to manhood. Inside, deep inside, I never believed I was fully male—I never believed I was growing up enough of a man. I believed that someplace out there, in other men, there was something that was genuine authentic all-American manhood—the real stuff—but I didn't have it: not enough of it to convince *me* anyway, even if I managed to be fairly convincing to those around me. I felt like an impostor, like a fake. I agonized a lot about not feeling male enough, and I had no idea then how much I was not alone.

Then I read those words—those words that suggested to me for the first time that the notion of manhood is a cultural delusion, a baseless belief, a false front, a house of cards. It's not true. The category I was trying so desperately to belong to, to be a member of in good standing—it doesn't exist. Poof. Now you see it, now you don't. Now you're terrified you're not really part of it; now you're free, you don't have to worry anymore. However removed you feel inside from "authentic manhood," it doesn't matter. What matters is the center inside yourself—and how you live, and how you treat people, and what you can contribute as you pass through life on this earth, and how honestly you love, and how carefully you make choices. Those are the things that really matter. Not whether you're a real man. There's no such thing.

The idea of the male sex is like the idea of an Aryan race. The Nazis believed in the idea of an Aryan race—they believed that the Aryan race really exists, physically, in nature—and they put a great deal of effort into making it real. The Nazis believed that from the blond hair and blue eyes occurring naturally in the human species, they could construe the existence of a separate *race*—a distinct category of human beings that was unambiguously rooted in the natural order of things. But traits do not a race make; traits only make traits. For the idea to be real that these physical traits comprised a race, the race had to be socially constructed. The Nazis inferiorized and exterminated those they defined as "non-Aryan." With that, the notion of an Aryan race began to seem to come true. That's how there could be a political entity known as an Aryan race, and that's how there could be for some people a personal, subjective sense that they belonged to it. This happened through hate and force, through violence and victimization, through treating millions of people as things, then exterminating them. The belief system shared by people who believed they were all Aryan could not exist apart from that force and violence. The force and violence created a racial class system, *and* it created those people's membership in the race considered "superior." The force and violence served their class interests in large part because it created and maintained the class itself. But the idea of an Aryan race could never become metaphysically true, despite all the violence unleashed to create it, because there simply *is* no Aryan race. There is only the idea of it—and the consequences of trying to make it seem real. The male sex is very like that.

Penises and ejaculate and prostate glands occur in nature, but the notion that these anatomical traits comprise a sex—a discrete class, separate and distinct, metaphysically divisible from some other sex, *the* "other sex"—is simply that: a notion, an idea. The penises exist; the male sex does not. The male sex is socially constructed. It is a political entity that flourishes only through acts of force and sexual terrorism. Apart from the global inferiorization and subordination of those who are defined as "nonmale," the idea of personal membership in the male sex class would have no recognizable meaning. It would make no sense. No one could be a member of it and no one would think they *should* be a member of it. There would be no male sex to belong to. That doesn't mean there wouldn't still be penises and ejaculate and prostate glands and such. It simply means that the center of our selfhood would not be required to reside inside an utterly fictitious category—a category that only seems real to the extent that those outside it are put down.

We live in a world divided absolutely into two sexes, even though nothing about human nature warrants that division. We are sorted into one category or another at birth based solely on a visual inspection of our groins, and the only question that's asked is whether there's enough elongated tissue around your urethra so you can pee standing up. The presence or absence of a long-enough penis is the primary criterion for separating who's to grow up male from who's to grow up female. And among all the ironies in that utterly whimsical and arbitrary selection process is the fact that *anyone* can pee both sitting down and standing up.

Male sexual identity is the conviction or belief, held by most people born with penises, that they are male and not female, that they belong to the male sex. In a society predicated on the notion that there are two "opposite" and "complementary" sexes, this idea not only makes sense, it *becomes* sense; the very idea of a male sexual identity produces sensation, produces the meaning of sensation, becomes the meaning of how one's body feels. The sense and the sensing of a male sexual identity is at once mental and physical, at once public and personal. Most people born with a penis between their legs grow up aspiring to feel and act unambiguously male, longing to belong to the sex that is male and daring not to belong to the sex that is not, and feeling this urgency for a visceral and constant verification of their male sexual identity—for a fleshy connection to manhood—as the driving force of their life. The drive does not originate in the anatomy. The sensations derive from the idea. The idea gives the feelings social meaning; the idea determines which sensations shall be sought.

People born with penises must strive to make the idea of male sexual identity personally real by doing certain deeds, actions that are valued and chosen because they produce the desired feeling of belonging to a sex that is male and not female. Male sexual identity is experienced only in sensation and action, in feeling and doing, in eroticism and ethics. The feeling of belonging to a male sex encompasses both sensations that are explicitly "sexual" and those that are not ordinarily regarded as such. And there is a tacit social value system according to which certain acts are chosen because they make an individual's sexedness feel real and certain other acts are eschewed because they numb it. That value system is the ethics of male sexual identity—and it may well be the social origin of all injustice.

Each person experiences the idea of sexual identity as more or less real, more or less certain, more or less true, depending on two very personal phenomena: one's feelings and one's acts. For many people, for instance, the act of fucking makes their sexual identity feel more real than it does at other times, and they can predict from experience that this feeling of greater certainty will last for at least a while after each time they fuck. Fucking is not the only such act, and not only so-called sex acts can result in feelings of certainty about sexual identity; but the act of fucking happens to be a very good example of the correlation between *doing* a specific act in a specific way and *sensing* the specificity of the sexual identity to which one aspires. A person can decide to do certain acts and not others just because some acts will have the payoff of a feeling of greater certainty about sexual identity and others will give the feedback of a feeling of less. The transient reality of one's sexual identity, a person can know, is always a function of what one does and how one's acts make one feel. The feeling and the act must conjoin for the idea of the sexual identity to come true. We all keep longing for surety of our sexedness that we can feel; we all keep striving through our actions to make the idea real.

In human nature, eroticism is not differentiated between "male" and "female" in any clear-cut way. There is too much of a continuum, too great a resemblance. From all that we know, the penis and the clitoris are identically "wired" to receive and retransmit sensations from throughout the body, and the congestion of blood within the lower torso during sexual excitation makes all bodies sensate in a remarkably similar manner. Simply put, we all share all the nerve and blood-vessel layouts that are associated with sexual arousal. Who can say, for instance, that the penis would not experience sensations the way that a clitoris does if this were not a world in which the penis is supposed to be hell-bent on penetration? By the time most men make it through puberty, they believe that erotic sensation is supposed to *begin* in their penis; that if engorgement has not begun there, then nothing else in their body will heat up either. There is a massive interior dissociation from sensations that do not explicitly remind a man that his penis is still there. And not only there as sensate, but *functional and operational.*

So much of most men's sexuality is tied up with gender-actualizing—with feeling like a real man—that they can scarcely recall an erotic sensation that had no gender-specific cultural meaning. As most men age, they learn to cancel out and deny erotic sensations that are not specifically linked to what they think a real man is supposed to feel. An erotic sensation unintentionally experienced in a receptive, communing mode—instead of in an aggressive and controlling and violative mode, for instance—can shut down sensory systems in an instant. An erotic sensation unintentionally linked to the "wrong" sex of another person can similarly mean sudden numbness. Acculturated male sexuality has a built-in fail-safe: Either its political context reifies manhood or the experience cannot be felt as sensual. Either the act creates his sexedness or it does not compute as a sex act. So he tenses up, pumps up, steels himself against the dread that he be found not male enough. And his dread is not stupid; for he sees what happens to people when they are treated as nonmales.

My point is that sexuality does not *have* a gender; it *creates* a gender. It creates for those who adapt to it in narrow and specified ways the confirmation for the individual of belonging to the idea of one sex or the other. So-called male sexuality is a learned connection between specific physical sensations and the idea of a male sexual identity. To achieve this male sexual identity requires that an individual *identify with* the class of males—that is, accept as one's own the values and interests of the class. A fully realized male sexual identity also requires *nonidentification with* that which is perceived to be nonmale, or female. A male must not identify with females; he must not associate with females in feeling, interest, or action. His identity as a member of the sex class men abso‑ lutely depends on the extent to which he repudiates the values and interests of the sex class "women."

I think somewhere inside us all, we have always known something about the relativity of gender. Somewhere inside us all, we know that our bodies harbor deep resemblances, that we are wired inside to respond in a profound harmony to the resonance of eroticism inside the body of someone near us. Physiologically, we are far more alike than different. The tissue structures that have become labial and clitoral or scrotal and penile have not forgotten their common ancestry. Their sensations are of the same source. The nerve networks and interlock of capillaries through-out our pelvises electrify and engorge as if plugged in together and pumping as one. That's what we feel when we feel one another's feel-ings. That's what can happen during sex that is mutual, equal, reciprocal, profoundly communing.

So why is it that some of us with penises think it's sexy to pressure someone into having sex against their will? Some of us actually get harder the harder the person resists. Some of us with penises actually believe that some of us without penises want to be raped. And why is it that some of us with penises think it's sexy to treat other people as objects, as things to be bought and sold, impersonal bodies to be possessed and consumed for our sexual pleasure? Why is it that some of us with penises are aroused by sex tinged with rape, and sex commoditized by pornog-raphy? Why do so many of us with penises want such antisexual sex?

There's a reason, of course. We have to make a lie seem real. It's a very big lie. We each have to do our part. Otherwise the lie will look like the lie that it is. Imagine the enormity of what we each must do to keep the lie alive in each of us. Imagine the awesome challenge we face to make the lie a social fact. It's a lifetime mission for each of us born with a penis: to have sex in such a way that the male sex will seem real—and so that we'll feel like a real part of it.

We all grow up knowing exactly what kind of sex that is. It's the kind of sex you can have when you pressure or bully someone else into it. So it's a kind of sex that makes your will more important than theirs. That kind of sex helps the lie a lot. That kind of sex makes you feel like someone important and it turns the other person into someone unimportant. That kind of sex makes you feel real, not like a fake. It's a kind of sex men have in order to feel like a real man.

There's also the kind of sex you can have when you force someone and hurt someone and cause someone suffering and humiliation. Violence and hostility in sex help the lie a lot too. Real men are aggressive in sex. Real men get cruel in sex. Real men use their penises like weapons in sex. Real men leave bruises. Real men think it's a turn-on to threaten harm. A brutish push can make an erection feel really hard. That kind of sex helps the lie a lot. That kind of sex makes you feel like someone who is powerful and it turns the other person into someone powerless. That kind of sex makes you feel dangerous and in control—like you're fighting a war with an enemy and if you're mean enough you'll win but if you let up you'll loose your manhood. It's a kind of sex men have *in order to have* a manhood.

There's also the kind of sex you can have when you pay your money into a profit system that grows rich displaying and exploiting the bodies and body parts of people without penises for the sexual entertainment of people with. Pay your money and watch. Pay your money and imagine. Pay your money and get real turned on. Pay your money and jerk off. That kind of sex helps the lie a lot. It helps support an industry committed to making people with penises believe that people without are sluts who just want to be ravished and reviled—an industry dedicated to maintaining a sex-class system in which men believe themselves sex machines and men believe women are mindless fuck tubes. That kind of sex helps the lie a lot. It's like buying Krugerrands as a vote of confidence for white supremacy in South Africa.

And there's one more thing: That kind of sex makes the lie indelible—burns it onto your retinas right adjacent to your brain—makes you remember it and makes your body respond to it and so it makes you believe that the lie is in fact true: You really are a real man. That slavish and submissive creature there spreading her legs is really not. You and that creature have nothing in common. That creature is an alien inanimate thing, but your penis is completely real and alive. Now you can come. Thank god almighty—you have a sex at last.

Now, I believe there are many who are sick at heart over what I have been describing. There are many who were born with penises who want to stop collaborating in the sex-class system that needs us to need these kinds of sex. I believe some of you want to stop living out the big lie, and you want to know how. Some of you long to touch truthfully. Some of you want sexual relationships in your life that are about intimacy and joy, ecstasy and equality—not antagonism and alienation. So what I have to say next I have to say to you.

When you use sex to have a sex, the sex you have is likely to make you feel crummy about yourself. But when you have sex in which you are not struggling with your partner in order to act out "real manhood," the sex you have is more likely to bring you close.

This means several specific things:

1. Consent is absolutely essential. If both you and your partner have not freely given your informed consent to the sex you are about to have, you can be quite certain that the sex you go ahead and have will make you strangers to each other. How do you know if there's consent? You ask. You ask again if you're sensing any doubt. Consent to do one thing isn't consent to do another. So you keep communicating, in clear words. And you don't take anything for granted.

2. Mutuality is absolutely essential. Sex is not something you do *to* someone. Sex is not a one-way transitive verb, with a subject, you, and an object, the body you're with. Sex that is mutual is not about doing and being done to; it's about being-with and feeling-with. You have to really be there to experience what is happening between and within the two of you—between every part of you and within both your whole bodies. It's a matter of paying attention—as if you are paying attention to someone who matters.

3. Respect is absolutely essential. In the sex that you have, treat your partner like a real person who, like you, has real feelings—feelings that matter as much as your own. You may or may not love—but you must always respect. You must respect the integrity of your partner's body. It is not yours for the taking. It belongs to someone real. And you do not get ownership of your partner's body just because you are having sex— or just because you have had sex.

For those who are closer to the beginning of your sex lives than to the middle or the end, many things are still changing for you about how you have sex, with whom, why or why not, what you like or dislike, what kind of sex you want to have more of. In the next few years, you are going to discover and decide a lot. I say "discover" because no one can tell you what you're going to find out about yourself in relation to sex— and I say "decide" because virtually without knowing it you are going to be laying down habits and patterns that will probably stay with you for the rest of your life. You're at a point in your sexual history that you will never be at again. You don't know what you don't know yet. And yet you are making choices whose consequences for your particular sexuality will be sealed years from now.

The Ethics of Male Sexual Identity

I speak to you as someone who is closer to the middle of my sexual history. As I look back, I see that I made many choices that I didn't know I was making. And as I look at men who are near my age, I see that what has happened to many of them is that their sex lives are stuck in deep ruts that began as tiny fissures when they were young. So I want to conclude by identifying what I believe are three of the most important decisions about your sexuality that you can make when you are at the beginning of your sexual history. However difficult these choices may seem to you now, I promise you they will only get more difficult as you grow older. I realize that what I'm about to give is some quite unsolicited nuts-and-bolts advice. But perhaps it will spare you, later on in your lives, some of the obsessions and emptiness that have claimed the sexual histories of many men just a generation before you. Perhaps it will not help, I don't know; but I hope very much that it will.

First, you can start choosing now not to let your sexuality be manipulated by the pornography industry. I've heard many unhappy men talk about how they are so hooked on pornography and obsessed with it that they are virtually incapable of a human erotic contact. And I have heard even more men talk about how, when they do have sex with someone, the pornography gets in the way, like a mental obstacle, like a barrier preventing a full experience of what's really happening between them and their partner. The sexuality that the pornography industry needs you to have is not about communicating and caring; it's about "pornographizing" people—objectifying and conquering them, not being with them as a person. You do not have to buy into it.

Second, you can start choosing now not to let drugs and alcohol numb you through your sex life. Too many men, as they age, become incapable of having sex with a clear head. But you need your head clear—to make clear choices, to send clear messages, to read clearly what's coming in on a clear channel between you and your partner. Sex is no time for your awareness to sign off. And another thing: Beware of relying on drugs or alcohol to give you "permission" to have sex, or to trick your body into feeling something that it's not, or so you won't have to take responsibility for what you're feeling or for the sex that you're about to have. If you can't take sober responsibility for your part in a sexual encounter, you probably shouldn't be having it—and you certainly shouldn't be zonked out of your mind *in order* to have it.

Third, you can start choosing now not to fixate on fucking—especially if you'd really rather have sex in other, noncoital ways. Sometimes men have coital sex—penetration and thrusting then ejaculating inside someone—not because they particularly feel like it but because they feel they *should* feel like it: It's expected that if you're the man, you fuck. And if you don't fuck, you're not a man. The corollary of this cultural imperative is that if two people don't have intercourse, they have not had real sex. That's baloney, of course, but the message comes down hard, especially inside men's heads: Fucking is *the* sex act, the act in which you act out what sex is supposed to be—and what sex you're supposed to be.

Like others born with a penis, I was born into a sex-class system that requires my collaboration every day, even in how I have sex. Nobody told me, when I was younger, that I could have noncoital sex and that it would be fine. Actually, much better than fine. Nobody told me about an incredible range of other erotic possibilities for mutual lovemaking—including rubbing body to body, then coming body to body; including multiple, nonejaculatory orgasms; including the feeling you get when even the tiniest place where you and your partner touch becomes like a window through which great tidal storms of passion ebb and flow, back and forth. Nobody told me about the sex you can have when you stop working at having a sex. My body told me, finally. And I began to trust what my body was telling me more than the lie I was supposed to make real.

I invite you too to resist the lie. I invite you too to become an erotic traitor to male supremacy.

Sexual Objectification and Male Supremacy

When a man looks at a person's body as if he wants that body to belong to him, or as if the body does belong to him—not as if the person is *somebody*, an independent, volitional person whose flesh belongs to that self only—and when a man looks at that body as if it were an object, a thing, and the man becomes sexually excited, what does that mean?

What does it mean that a man becomes sexually aroused when he looks at a body in that way, and what does it mean that he looks at a body in that way *in order* to become sexually aroused?

When a man is in a public place, and he sees a person from some distance, a person whom he has never seen before, and he applies his attention to the person's body, and he scrutinizes the person's body with a particular intensity, with deliberate curiosity, with unequivocal intent, and inside his body there begins a pounding, a rushing of blood, a craving, and what he craves is to have sex with that stranger, what does that mean?

What does it mean when a man is in a darkened theater, watching a film, and he is watching pictures of a performer who has a certain appearance and behaves in a certain way, and he studies that body through the performer's clothing, and the image of the performer's body, the shape of it, its softness and solidity, the definition of its sexedness, is more real, more present to him at that moment than any other aspect of his conscious life, and in gazing at that image he feels more urgently virile, more intensely connected to his manhood, than he feels in relation to any actual person, what does that mean?

When with one hand a man is paging through a magazine, a magazine containing photographs of naked and nearly naked bodies, bodies posed with their genitals concealed and bodies posed with their genitals showing, bodies posed with props and with other bodies, bodies posed with their faces looking at the camera and not looking at the camera, bodies posed by a photographer to look available, accessible, takeable, in color and in black and white, and with his other hand the man is masturbating, and he is searching from picture to picture, searching from body to body, from part of body to part of body, from pose to pose, rhythmically stroking and squeezing and straining, seeking some coalescence of the flesh he is looking at and the sensations in his own, imagining his body and one of the bodies attached, joined, tenderly or forcefully, and he masturbates until he is finished, and when he is done he is done looking, and he stores them away until next time, the magazines, the pictures, the bodies, the parts of bodies, what does that mean?

When a man stands at a magazine rack, and his eyes roam from image to image, from photograph to photograph, pausing over the bodies that make him palpitate the most, the bodies that make his insides sensate, the way a great and sudden fright does, the way a sonic boom does, the particular bodies that astonish him, that jolt him, that make him tremble with sexual longing, exacerbating an ache, a pelvic congestion that never seems to leave him, bodies that he can count on to do that, bodies that will be there to do that when that is what he needs done, and the magazines that are not wrapped in plastic he opens, he thumbs through, until he finds the ones that are effective, the ones he wants at home, and he takes some, he buys some, what does that mean?

When in order to feel like having sex, a man requires sex partners who look a certain way, who have a certain build, and when as they age he discards them, and when as he ages he becomes increasingly obsessed with obtaining sex partners who are the specific body type, the color, the age that he requires, and he obtains them however he can, by buying them, by buying pictures of them, by owning them somehow, what does that mean?

When a man is in a public place and he observes a particular person, a person he has never seen before or a person he sees there regularly, a person whose body triggers his sexual curiosity, and he seeks out opportunities for surveillance, obviously or discreetly, to look at a part of the body in more detail, or several parts, or to see the person less clothed, or to be nearer to the person so as to touch, brush against, press next to, or grasp, and he remembers the body that he has seen, he memorizes its details, the particular shapes of its sexual parts, and the memory continues in him vividly, in his imagining, during his subsequent episodes of sexual arousal, alone or with someone else, and he carries that picture with him, that picture and the pictures he has taken in his mind of other strangers' bodies, and they stay with him, they are his, and he reviews the pictures mentally, and the reviewing helps him come, what does that mean?

What does it mean when a man calls up pictures in his mind when he is having sex with someone's body, in order to imagine a different body, a body that is not there, pictures of a body that suits him, a body he thinks about in his mind in order to feel like having sex?

When a man is feeling tense or angry or anxious, or withdrawn and isolated and irritable and unhappy with himself, and so to make himself feel better he has sex by himself, with pictures of other people's bodies in his mind, with pictures of other people's bodies in his hand, pictures of particular parts and poses, and as he masturbates he uses the photographed or mental pictures to help him imagine a body there with him, a particular body he can seem to be with, to touch and feel, a body he can do things to, a body to connect to, an imaginary body more real than his own, and the more vividly he imagines the body the more aroused he becomes, until he comes, having sex in his mind with a body in a picture, and he feels a moment's relaxation and resolution, a fleeting consolation, then, gradually or suddenly, he feels unease again, disconsolate, incomplete and cut off, and the body he had imagined has vanished, there's nobody else there, and he doesn't *want* anybody else there, he wants to be utterly alone now far more than he had wanted to have sex with someone before, what does that mean?

What does it mean that a man's most routine, most repeated, most reliable, perhaps even most intensely "personal" erotic experiences are those that happen in relation to things, to bodies perceived and regarded as things, to images depicting bodies as things, to memories of images of bodies as things? What does it mean that he responds sexually to bodies as things and images of bodies as things in a way that is more or less constant, no matter whether another human being is actually with him? What does it mean when a man's inner life is obsessionally devoted to his sexual objectifying? What does it mean when a man arranges much of his life around his sexual objectifying, to make sure he will periodically and often be in circumstances where he can become sexually aroused in relation to bodies he imagines as things? What does it mean that a man's appetites, attention, opinions, and buying habits have become almost completely manipulable simply by triggering his habit of sexual objectifying? What does it mean that in his sexual responsiveness to his sexual objectifying, such a man is quite ordinary? What does it mean that such a man is "normal"?

44

Sexual Objectifying as an Act

Of course, not all men's *selections* of sexual objects are considered normal. There is much psychiatric, religious, and legal disagreement over which sets of parts or body types a man is entitled to sexually objectify. From various points of view, various sexual objects are taboo: depending upon their gender; depending upon their age; depending upon their color, creed, or class; depending upon how much force or violence the man wants to use against them in fantasy or in fact; depending upon which sex acts he wants to perform, which genitals and orifices he wants conjoined; depending upon whether another man has a prior claim to exclusive possession of the sexual object; and so on. But sexual objectification in and of itself is considered the norm of male sexuality. Men's sexual objectifying is deemed a given, a biological mandate, having the same preordained relationship to male sexual responsiveness that, say, the smelling of food has to a ravenous person's salivation. Men's sexual objectifying—apart from hair-splitting quibbles about which sex objects are inappropriate—is seen as a "natural" and "healthy" way of looking at other people. In fact, sexual objectifying is considered to be as natural as the sense of sight itself: Typically, men believe that whenever one is responding sexually to visual stimuli, one must by definition be sexually objectifying, despite the obvious fact that vision is not at all essential for sexual objectification to occur (after all, it can happen with the lights out; and, for that matter, someone blind from birth can regard another person as a sex object, as a thing). Male sexuality without sexual objectification is unimagined. Male sexuality without it would not be male sexuality. So of course there is never inquiry into the *activity* itself, the actual *doing* that is sexual objectification. What is the act that is done and how is it done—and what are its consequences? If all we know about sexual objectification is that when a man does it he becomes sexually aroused, perhaps to climax, then we really don't know a lot, because we really don't yet know anything about the process, the dynamic, the event, the sense in which "to sexually objectify" is a *verb*. To probe the matter further, we don't yet know anything about the *ethical meaning* of the act: In what sense is it *intransitive*—merely a private and perhaps inconsequential mental event—or in what sense it is *transitive*—a transaction in which there is a *doer*, a *deed*, someone the deed is *done to*, and certain *consequences*, which should and can be evaluated?

Needless to say, trying to delineate the ethical meaning of sexual objectification is very difficult. On the one hand, there is no tradition of public and truthful discourse about men's sexual response to their perception and treatment of people as objects. There is scarcely even a vocabulary. And on the other hand, trying to think about sexual objectification in a conscientious way can make the mind want to give up, go blank, and shut down. Trying to unlock and unblock the function of sexual objectifying in a man's life and trying to trace the effects of sexual objectification, particularly on women's lives, can be to risk recognizing too much that is too deeply disturbing. Trying to think about the reality and experience of sexual objectification can be like struggling to untie a knot that has been pulled too tight over too many years by too many hands—and like having one's own fingers bound up someplace in the knot.

There are much easier ways of discussing sexual objectification—types of discourse in which troublesome questions of ethical responsibility need not arise. For instance, a natural scientist can speak of evolution and genetics in terms that provide social scientists with a vocabulary for rendering the function of sexual objectification ethically neutral. A zoologist can state that sexual objectification serves an evolutionary purpose in the natural order, in the selection of mating partners who will improve the species. An anthropologist can state that sexual objectification in humans is analogous to the way animals respond to one another's odors, especially pheromones released during estrus. And a sociobiologist can state that there is a genetic basis for sexual objectification: It is an expression of our DNA and its hell-bent drive to be present at the conception of the next generation's gene pool. In such ways as these, one can discourse with ease, and one can evade the ethical issues entirely.

Evaluation of the ethical issues in men's sexual behavior has fallen on hard times. It is the fashion nowadays to presume that an act is more or less outside the pale of ethical examination if at any point along the course of it there is an erection or an ejaculation. It is also the fashion to describe human conduct in language that obscures the fact of acts, the fact that acts have consequences, and the fact that one is connected to one's acts whether or not one acknowledges it. Also, it is fashionable to call acts "reactions," as if the agent really responsible for the act were someone or something else. So it is that in matters of men's sexual behavior there is talk of "feelings," "emotional reactions," "expression," and "fantasies" in situations where it would be more accurate to speak of actions that are *actions*—that is, susceptible to ethical interpretation and evaluation: Who is doing exactly what to whom? is the act fair or unfair? what is the consequence of the act for the person to whom it is done? and is the person who is doing the act paying any attention to the act, its consequence, and its impact on someone else? This sort of ethical interpretation is not synonymous with ascribing "sinfulness" or "righteousness" or "damnation" or "beatitude." Such lofty categories—which hang by a thread from supremely suspect cosmologies—are rarely clear ways of articulating matters of nitty-gritty justice between human selves. Rather, to inquire into the ethical meaning of sexual objectification is to attempt to identify that aspect of sexual objectifying which is a transitive *doing*— an act that someone does, an act that someone does to someone else as if to some thing. Just because the act treats another person as not a real person does not mean there is no real person to whom the act is done. To be sure, technology today can significantly change the time and space continuity in which acts of sexual objectification and their consequences might ordinarily be considered to have a connection. For instance, the act of sexually objectifying the body of someone who is actually "there," actually alive and present to the one who is doing the sexual objectifying, may have a somewhat different ethical meaning from the act of sexually objectifying someone whose body is now represented in a photograph or film (which exists as documentary evidence that an act of sexual objectification was done to a particular person at some other time and place by someone else). Nevertheless, both acts have an ethical meaning. Someone—the one who is doing the objectifying—is doing something, and what he is doing is an act—he is not simply reacting, he is not simply into a feeling state, he is not simply expressing his sexuality, he is not simply having a fantasy. And whatever his feelings, reactions, expression, or imaginings, they do not disconnect his act from its impact on other selves.

When a man sexually objectifies someone—that is, when he regards another person's body as a thing, not another self, for the purpose of his own subjective sexual stimulation—he is not terribly likely to be perceptive of what is happening to anyone other than himself. Actually, the man is likely to be completely oblivious to what is happening to the person he is objectifying, because once he objectifies that person—once he reduces the person in his mind to the object he desires—then the person, to him, is by definition not a real *subject* like himself. If he considers his objectifying to have any effect at all, he may project onto the person a rather asinine reveling in what he is doing; and indeed, the person objectified may be duped into feeling "flattered" at having been singled out for a particular man's depersonalization—a dubious distinction often confused with being "desired." But to him, this person is not worth any real empathy at all because this person simply does not exist as someone who could have a valid experience apart from, much less contrary to, his own. "What is happening" is his own sexual arousal, period. Given his subjective self-absorption at this point, in his own mind there is literally no real other self present to whom anything *could* be happening.

Sexually objectifying a person makes them seem absent, not really "there" as an equally real self, whether or not the person is physically present. In this way, the one who is sexually objectifying interposes a distance between himself and the person he sexually objectifies; it is a gulf between someone who experiences himself as real and someone whom he experiences as not-real. Then, if while sexually objectifying he proceeds to have sex, either alone or "with someone," he experiences the reality of his sexual arousal and release as a mediator, a sensory go-between, which produces a transient feeling of what seems to him like personal, sexual intimacy. But it is essentially a solipsistic event, a completely self-referential sexual experience.

Men's predisposition to sexually objectify, combined with modern image-making technologies, has created a vast commerce in photographic documents of people being turned into things. The camera has become both medium and metaphor for men's sexual objectification: It can be used to take a picture of an actual person being sexually objectified, then the image can be duplicated and sold to millions of men so they can vicariously be sexually "present" to the body of the person made "absent" in the picture. In this way, the consumer is connected—both viscerally and ethically—to the act of sexual objectification that took place in front of the camera. The picture is taken the way it is taken so that it can be sold the way it is sold so that it can be used the way it is used. Each consumer, each purchaser of a reproduced documentation of the original sexual objectification, is complicitous in the commerce, a link in the chain of profit, and hence he bears some responsibility, however widely shared by others, for the act of sexual objectification that took place in front of the camera to begin with, even though it happened before he paid. The act was not done *by* him, but as soon as he buys a documentation of it he becomes someone it was done *for*, someone whose intent—along with that of many others—was collectively expressed and acted out in the original, particular act. Knowing that he shares this intent with other men—a class of consumers who are similarly situated, both viscerally and ethically, vis-à-vis the person pictured—is in fact a significant element in the "pleasure" he receives; and his identification with those other men's subjectivity is the extent to which his perceptions are even remotely empathic. When men—individually and collectively—have sex looking at a photographed sex object, they are literally having sex with a thing, the photograph, and they are figuratively having sex with the thing that a photographer has turned someone into. The whole point of consuming documentations of sexual objectification is *not* to empathize with the person who is being objectified. To call this mass-marketed necrophilia is only a slight exaggeration; in differing degrees, men who sexually objectify through pictures tend to respond to images of "ecstasy," "wantonness," and sexual accessibility that are actually photographed signs of *lifelessness*: Certain druggy and drowsy facial expressions, postures of languidness bordering on paralysis, dull eyes that stare off emptily into space—these are all popular symbols—or, perhaps more accurately, commonplace symptoms—of a cancelled-out consciousness, an absence of self-possessed selfhood, a lack of independent volition, a kind of brain death.

Male Supremacy and Male Selfhood

How does a man's history of sexual objectifying begin? Toward whom? in what context? and why? There are doubtless as many different details as there are individual men, but all men's psychosexual histories share a set of common themes because all men's psychosexual histories occur within male supremacy.

Male supremacy is the honest term for what is sometimes hedgingly called patriarchy. It is the social system of rigid dichotomization by gender through which people born with penises maintain power in the culture over and against the sex caste of people who were born without penises. Male supremacy is not rooted in any natural order; rather, it has been socially constructed, socially created, especially through a socially constructed belief in what a sex is, how many there are, and who belongs to which.

Sexual objectification has a crucial relationship to male supremacy. Sexual objectification is not rooted in the natural order of things either; rather, sexual objectification is a habit that develops because it has an important function in creating, maintaining, and expressing male supremacy. The relationship of sexual objectification to male supremacy works in two mutually reinforcing ways: (1) Men's habit of sexually objectifying serves in part to construct the male supremacy of culture, and (2) the male supremacy of culture urges males to adapt by adopting the habit of sexually objectifying. This habit becomes as strong as it does in each man's lifetime precisely because the habit serves most forcefully to locate his sense of himself as a peer in relation to the supremacy he perceives in other males. Once he knows that location palpably, he knows what can be called a male sexual identity—a sense of himself as having dissociated sufficiently from the inferior status of females.

Here's how the habit emerges: First, there comes a time in the life of the child-with-a-penis when it dawns on him that his world is organized into two discrete categories of people—male and female, or however he conceptualizes them at the time. Somewhat later he realizes, through social cues of varying weight, that he had better identify with one (male) and disidentify with the other (Mom). There also comes a time when he experiences this state of affairs and his own precarious relationship to it with no small measure of confusion, stress, anxiety, and fear. Call this his gender-identity anxiety—his particular terror about not completely identifying as male. (Of course, boy children are not actually on record about this point, but it is an inference that can reasonably be drawn from memory and observation.) Next, there comes a time in the course of the growth of his body when various conditions of risk, peril, hazard, and threat cause his penis to become erect—without his understanding why and without, as yet, any particular sexual content. (This much is not conjecture; it has been documented in interviews with prepubescent boys.[1]) Among the events or experiences that boys report as being asso-ciated with erections are accidents, anger, being scared, being in danger, big fires, fast bicycle riding, fast sled riding, hearing a gunshot, playing or watching exciting games, boxing and wrestling, fear of punishment, being called on to recite in class, and so on. Call this his basic fight-or-flight reflex, involuntarily expressed at that age as an erection. The catch is, of course, that this humble flurry of anatomical activity just happens to occur in the context of a society that prizes the penis not only as the locus of male sexual identity but also as the fundamental determinant of all sacred and secular power. Call this, therefore, feedback from the boy's body that is loaded with male-supremacist portent, to say the least.[2]

In his early years, a young male's involuntary "nonsexual" erections (those that arise from peril, for instance, as against touch and warmth) can be so distracting and disconcerting that they trigger even more panic and anxiety, which in turn can make detumescence quite impossible. At some point in his life, if he is developing "normally," he learns a physical and emotional association between this dread and his "desire"; this is the point when, perhaps irrevocably, his gender anxiety and his reflex erec-tions become linked: In relation to other people's bodies, he experiences acutely his anxiety about his identification with authentic maleness—particularly in relation to those details of other people's bodies that he perceives as gender-specific. Somewhere in the moment of his perceiv-ing what he regards as another body's unambiguous sexedness, he experiences a jolt, an instant of panic, a synapse of dread, as if reminded that his own authenticity as a man hangs in the balance. The panic, the physiological agitation, produces an automatic erection. He eventually learns to desire such erections because he experiences them as a *reso-lution* of his gender anxiety, at least temporarily—because while he is feeling them, he is feeling most profoundly a sensory affiliation with what he infers to be the sexedness of other men. Nevertheless, he continues to depend upon his gender anxiety as a source of the physical and emotional agitation that he knows can be counted on, if properly stimulated, to make his penis hard.*

The Promise of Violence

Sexual objectifying in people born with penises is a learned response in a social context that is male-supremacist. Male sexual objectifying is not biologically ordained, or genetically determined. Rather, the male supremacy of culture determines how penile sensations will be interpreted. The meaning of those sensations becomes variously encoded and imprinted over time, such that a male will develop a characteristic habit of responding with an erection to his perceiving of gender specificity in other bodies. In his quest for more reliable repetition of such erections, he may cultivate a private iconography of gender-specific bodies and body parts, particular emblems of gender dichotomy that revive his buried anxiety about whether he really belongs to the sex he is supposed to. The particular iconography may vary greatly from man to man—for example, the emblematic body images may be predominantly female, in which case his objectifying is deemed heterosexual, or the images may be predominantly male, in which case his objectifying is deemed homosexual. In any case, all male sexual objectifying originates in the common predicament of how to identify and feel real as a male in a male-supremacist culture. The predicament can be resolved either in contradistinction to a female object or through assimilation of a male object. Either way, the resolution strived for is a body-bond with men.

Male sexual objectifying is not simply a response to male supremacy;

---

* The elective "forbiddenness" of homosexual encounters, as for instance in public places, and the objective physical danger of many sadistic sex practices can also be seen to preserve the role of risk, peril, hazard, and threat in effectively inducing erections.

---

it functions to enforce male supremacy as well. Everywhere one looks—whether in mass culture or high culture—there are coded expressions of male sexual objectification—primarily presentations of women and girls as objects—displayed like territorial markings that define the turf as a world to be seen through men's eyes only. There are some constraints on male sexual objectifying of other males; most men do not want done to them what men are supposed to do to women. Meanwhile most women find their economic circumstances determined to a large extent by whether and for how many years their physical appearance meets standards laid down by men—standards that both heterosexual and homosexual men conspire to decree. And for many women, male sexual objectification is a prelude to sexual violence.

Sometimes the mere regarding of another person's body as an object is not enough; it does not satisfy a man's habituated need to experience physical and emotional agitation sufficient to set off sensory feedback about his sexedness. At times like these, a man learns, he can reproduce the erectile result of feeling threat, terror, and danger as a child simply by being threatening, terrifying, and dangerous to his chosen sex object. It works even better now, because now he is in control. He can successfully do this in his imagination, then in his life, then again in his memory, then again in his life. . . . It works even better now; the more dread he produces, the more "desire" he can feel.

Before a man commits a sexual assault or a forced sex act, that man performs an act of sexual objectification: He makes a person out to be an object, a thing less real than himself, a thing with a sex; he regards that object as sexual prey, a sexual target, a sexual alien—in order that he can fully feel his own reality as a man. Not all sexual objectifying necessarily precedes sexual violence, and not all men are yet satiated by their sexual objectifying; but there is a perceptible sense in which every act of sexual objectifying occurs on a continuum of dehumanization that promises male sexual violence at its far end. The depersonalization that begins in sexual objectification is what makes violence possible; for once you have made a person out to be a thing, you can do anything to it you want.

Finally, the dirty little secret about sexual objectification is that it is an act that cannot be performed with any attention to its ethical meaning. Experientially—from the point of view of a man who is sexually objectifying—sexual objectification and ethical self-awareness are mutually exclusive: A man cannot reflect on what he is doing and its real consequences for real people and at the same time fully accomplish the act of sexual objectifying. There's no way it can be done, because his own subjective reality is too contingent upon the *un*reality of someone else. All that can be left "out there" in his field of awareness is the other person's sexedness—an abstract representation of a gender—in comparison with which his own sexedness may flourish and engorge. So it is that a man shuts off his capacity for ethical empathy—whatever capacity he may ever have had—in order to commit an act of depersonalization that is "gratifying" essentially because it functions to fulfill his sense of a selfhood that is authentically male.

If there is ever to be any possibility of sexual equality in anyone's lifetime, it requires, minimally, both the capacity and the commitment to regard another person as a whole self, as someone who has an integrity of independent and autonomous experience, as someone who is, simply, just as real as oneself. But as a society we are as far from realizing that requisite in matters of private sexual behavior as we are in matters of public policy. When private sexual arousal becomes predicated on imagining that a particular other person is *not* real, not there, not an inhabitant of his or her body as an equally active subject; when most of the sex that men have takes place between their own imagined reality and their so-called partner's imaged unreality; when completely self-referential orgasmic release can pass for "a meaningful sexual relationship"; when private sexual objectification has become tacit public policy, our agreed-upon criterion of "liberated" sexuality; when the consumer market is saturated with pictorial documentations of sexual objectification specifically merchandised for men's use in masturbation, for repetitive conditioning of their sexuality to respond to alienation from other people's real lives . . . it means that all of us are in deep trouble.

The ethical issues in any sexual relating are complex and varied. There may perhaps be no way to be absolutely certain that one is acting completely fairly or responsibly in any particular sexual encounter. We are, as the saying goes, "only human." But our shared humanity does not obviate our obligation to try; on the contrary, it is what *creates* our obligation: because *all* of us are human. In sexual objectification, we suspend our belief that that is true, and we violate our mutual rights to reality. But there's also a sense in which we cut ourselves off from our own human individuality, because we cut ourselves off from our responsibility for our acts. Responsibility is personal; it is who we are. We disappear to one another as persons when we cancel out our personal responsibility; we disconnect, we lose hold; we stop interacting as subject and subject. The way out of our insularity is not as subject and object, nor as taker and taken, nor as real-self and sex-toy. That's not intimacy; that's merely adjacency. What connects us, what relates us, is our certainty that each of us is real—and how we take that profound fact into account in whatever, together, we do.

Part II

The Politics of Male Sexual Identity

Eroticism and Violence in the Father-Son Relationship

No one can really understand how men treat women without understanding how men treat other men—and no one can really understand how men treat other men without understanding how men treat women. The father-son relationship is usually a boy's first exposure to this complex interlock of sexual politics. The lessons he learns in this relationship last a lifetime, and they become the basis of all he ever believes to be true about who he is supposed to be in relation to women and to other men.

Beyond being a personal and biographical experience, the father-son relationship is an element of culture that replicates and reproduces many of society's most fundamental sexual-political values. So it seems crucial to me to analyze that relationship in depth—both from the political perspective of radical feminism[1] and from the personal perspective of one who has grown up as a son.

In the three sections that follow, I look first at the *context* of the father-son relationship, then at its *content*, and finally at its *consequences*.

The Context

Patriarchy, also known as father right, is the sexual-political context of the father-son relationship. Indeed, father right is the cultural context of *all* relationships between humans.

One remarkable aspect of father right is the quantity of violence required to enforce it, the quantity of violence required to perpetuate it, to keep it the form in which humans live out their lives, the air they breathe so long as they inhale and exhale. If father right were natural, or inevitable, or inherent in human biology, one might have thought that so much coercion would not be necessary—and so many would not be suffocating.

Father right is now the most widespread form of social organization on the planet. The Random House Dictionary defines *patriarchy* as "a form of social organization in which the father is the supreme authority in the family, clan, or tribe and descent is reckoned in the male line, with the children belonging to the father's clan or tribe." This definition of patriarchy is certainly patriarchal—it neglects to mention the children's mother. Her body, it should be noted, belongs to the father first. The father possesses her, legally and carnally; the verb "to possess" indicates literally what he does to her. That is why and that is how all children under father right belong to fathers, not to mothers.

Many would like to believe that father right is morally neutral, simply an ingenious and equitable human invention of kinship that is necessitated by the composition of zygotes—so that a person who contributes a sperm cell and a person who contributes an egg cell might know with equal certainty who is related to whom genetically. But father right is not so simple, father right is not so scientific, nor is father right an expression of gender justice in any way.

Fundamentally, father right is a system of ownership, literal ownership of other human lives—ownership of the labor, will, body, and consciousness of whole other people, whole human beings. And that ownership begins with ownership by adult men of the only means of producing those lives, the flesh and blood of women.

Patriarchal law *legalizes* that ownership. Normal phallic eroticism *embodies* that ownership. Patriarchal culture also romanticizes, spiritualizes, emotionalizes, and psychologizes the right of men to own women and children as property. Patriarchal culture tends to obscure the violence in those structures of human relationship that are essentially structures of possession, as of inanimate objects. But it is in patriarchal law and phallic eroticism that father right is fixed and father right is felt. The law and the phallus are both primary instruments of owning.

The reality of male ownership in all human relationships under father right can be seen immediately and most clearly as it affects the lives of humans defined by culture as female—all humans, that is, who were born without a penis. At no time in a woman's life is she not defined by law and culture as the actual or potential property of someone who is male, someone born *with* a penis. First, as a child, she is owned by a father, the man who owns the flesh of her mother in marriage. That man owns her as a daughter until such time as her body is contracted into marriage—until she is possessed carnally and legally by a husband.

The modern western marriage custom of a father's "giving away the bride" is a remnant from the time when the father sold his daughter for money. This commodity exchange, the bride price paid by a husband to a father, continued in Europe until shortly after the Crusades, when a lot of men had died and the bottom dropped out of the bride market. According to the economics of supply and demand, the bride price was abandoned and fathers began to give their daughters away for free. To this day, the marriage ceremony is a ritual reminder that title to a woman's body has been transferred from one male owner to another.

Under common law, a husband cannot be charged with rape if he did it to his wife; she is his property; he can do to his property whatever he pleases.[2] Historically, rape was recognized as a crime only against the male owner of property. If the woman who was raped was still the virgin daughter of a father, the law recognized the rape as a crime against the father whose property was devalued. If the woman who was raped was the married wife of a husband, the law recognized the rape as a crime against the husband whose property was stolen. Rape exposes the reality that female flesh is never her own. If at some time in her life it is not the carnal property of a father or husband, she still has no claim to it; it belongs to any man who wants it. To this day, in any court of law, a woman who is not married, who is also no longer the virgin daughter of a father, faces cruel societal censure if she claims that a man committed a sex act against her body and will. The underlying presumption is that such a sex act is not a real crime, since no particular man owns her, therefore no actual party has been aggrieved. And to this day, any woman who is raped also faces hysterical* rejection and abuse by any man who regularly fucks her. Though he may or may not legally own her body in marriage, he has felt that he owns it while fucking, and he no longer can function with the same feeling since his personal property was defiled.

Patriarchal law both protects and expresses a cultural norm of phallic eroticism. Normally acculturated phallic eroticism responds best and basically to bodies as objects, to human flesh as property. Phallic eroticism is intrinsically proprietorial; it is an eroticism cultivated for owning, and it is dysfunctional and insensate except in relation to human flesh

---

* According to the Random House Dictionary, the word *hysteria* means "an uncontrollable outburst of emotion or fear, often characterized by irrationality." The word *hysteria* derives from the Greek, where it meant, literally, "suffering of the womb." Perhaps the word should be spelled *histeria*, to denote the suffering of the proprietorial penis.

---

perceived and treated as personal property. Phallic eroticism is intrinsically alienating; it is an eroticism cultivated for defending the barrier between subject and object, active and passive, owner and owned, master and slave. Phallic eroticism is intrinsically hostile, for violence is necessary to sustain such an unnatural relationship to other human life. By defining men's property rights to the bodies of women, patriarchal law licenses and reinforces each man's private eroticized owning, each man's private eroticized estranging, each man's private eroticized violence. And patriarchal law seeks to protect each man's erotic privacy from usurpation by other men.

According to human biology, only a woman can birth a child; a child not birthed by a mother does not, in nature, exist. According to patriarchal law, however, a child not owned by a man is deemed a legal nonentity and is called "illegitimate" or "bastard," because the law grants men exclusively the right to ownership of children. A woman who is not properly owned by a man when she gives birth to a child is scorned, shamed, humiliated, and castigated; and an unwed mother who persists in birthing children that are not a father's property may be forced against her will to be sterilized. In order to make certain that men will own every child that women birth, all the forces of law and culture are allied to keep every woman's body the legal and carnal property of men throughout her life.

Male ownership of children has always been separate and distinct from the labor of human custodianship. If a woman is properly owned by a man when she gives birth to a child, among her duties to the man is to act as custodian of his child. That means feeding it and cleaning up after it, disposing of the enormous quantity of shit, for instance, that an infant produces in the first three years of its life. That shit-work is custodial. It is not an owner's duty. A properly owned mother literally takes care of children that are legally, always, the human property of a father.

Historically, it was a dead father's legal right to have bequeathed his children to another man, irrespective of the fact that his wife (the children's mother) might still be alive. Elizabeth Cady Stanton, addressing the Joint Judiciary Committee of the New York State Legislature in 1854, described the legal prerogative of fathers at that time:

The father may apprentice his child, bind him out to a trade, without the mother's consent—yea, in direct opposition to her most earnest entreaties, prayers and tears. . . . Moreover, the father, about to die, may bind out all his children wherever and to whomsoever he may see fit, and thus, in fact, will away the guardianship of all his children from the mother. . . . Thus, by your laws, the child is the absolute property of the father, wholly at his disposal in life or at death.[3]

Four years later, as a direct consequence of action by the first U.S. Women's Rights Movement, the New York State Legislature passed a law declaring every married woman "the joint guardian of her children, with her husband, with equal powers, rights and duties in regard to them, with the husband."[4] This law was called the Married Women's Property Act of 1860; and it applied significantly to mothers who were widowed, for it guaranteed that they could continue custodianship of a dead father's children. This statute was the first legal challenge in history to a precept upon which all of patriarchal culture stands, the principle that human lives can be controlled by a father who is dead. The power of male ownership from the grave is still alive and well, of course, not only in patriarchal law and the Judeo-Christian religious tradition, but also in personal psychological identity. As Juliet Mitchell has observed:

Whether or not the actual father is there does not affect the perpetuation of the patriarchal culture within the psychology of the individual; present or absent, "the father" always has his place. His actual absence may cause confusion, or, on another level, relief, but the only difference it makes is within the terms of the over-all patriarchal assumption of his presence. In our culture he is just as present in his absence.[5]

So-called child-custody disputes are a rather recent historical phenomenon. In that same speech to the New York State Legislature, Elizabeth Cady Stanton described this situation of mothers:

In case of separation, the law gives the children to the father; no matter what his character or condition. At this very time we can point you to noble, virtuous, well-educated mothers in this State, who have abandoned their husbands for their profligacy and confirmed drunkenness. All these have been robbed of their children, who are in the custody of the husband, under the care of his relatives, whilst the mothers are permitted to see them but at stated intervals.... [6]

The laws on divorce—as to what are its proper grounds, for instance—were framed then as now in the interests of fathers. But those interests have shifted somewhat. Only within the last several decades did it become in the father's interest to allow an extension of the mother's custodial responsibilities to his children after terminating, in divorce, her domestic and coital responsibilities to him. The father's ownership of his children could thus be maintained at a comfortable and convenient distance, without the burden on him of finding someone to do the shit-work. This recent history is reflected in the few remaining "maternal preference" state laws, which automatically continue custodianship of children by divorced mothers, but only those children who are yet very young.

A pendulum of paternal pride has swung, however, and fathers are again rejecting divorced mothers as suitable custodians for their children.[7] Custodianship is not ownership. Custodianship is service, shit-work, and daily care. Ownership is the legal relationship of a father to his child, a relationship of owner to human property that is immutable, even in death. Modern child-custody disputes reveal how all mother-child relationships under father right become distorted and deformed according to the model of the property relationship that obtains between father and child. In a child-custody dispute, the mother must now haggle on the father's turf (the court) and in the father's terms (children as property). And the unnatural question to be resolved is who shall "own" this child's time and company, this child's affection and allegiance—discounting the custodial labor the mother performed for that child's life, since that labor was a function of the father's former ownership of *her*.

Phallic eroticism entirely informs these disputes. In order to be permitted to continue her custodial relationship to a father's children, the divorced mother must pass a peculiar test as to whether or not she is "fit." That test, essentially, is celibacy, a test supported by much contemporary legal opinion. In order to continue her labor of custodianship toward a father's children, the divorced mother must demonstrate to the court that she has not improperly become the carnal possession of another man. If she must return to court years later—in the likely event, for instance, that the father has stopped sending her money to support the child—she may again be required to pass the celibacy test of "fitness." The use of money by fathers to control the lives of ex-wives and children is a custom protected by law. And the celibacy test for divorced mothers assures the father in his imagination that his ex-wife, like a daughter, will stay carnally owned by him until such time as another man legally marries her. The courts recognize the prerogative of that father's imagination not to be perturbed. Of course, even more perturbing than carnal possession of the mother by another man is the case of a divorced mother who would share her eroticism with a woman. In a child-custody dispute, a mother's lesbianism is deemed worse than adultery. The hysteria of a father whose private property has been violated by the penis of another man is exceeded by the hysteria of a father whose former private property has renounced phallic possession altogether. The courts, needless to say, protect a father from all such hysteria under the camouflage of what is best for the "welfare" of his child.

Just as father right is predicated on the right of absent and dead fathers to own and control the living, so also is father right predicated on the right of living fathers to own and control the unborn. Nowhere in America is abortion available to women free and on demand; in many states where abortion has been decriminalized, the consent of the nearest male relative must be obtained, or there must be a second attending physician to try to save the fetus. Patriarchal law protects the property relationship of a father to his fetus. That law expresses the erotic relationship between a man and his phallus. Fathers fantasize all fetuses as male, and, in effect, as repositories of phallic life. Acculturated phallic eroticism is genital-centric; all sense of life is centered in the phallus; the rest of the body is armored and kept relatively dead. The phallus thus seems to have an independent life and will of its own, autonomous and unpredictable, and the man is at pains to control it, to make it do what he wants. Least of all does he want it to be cut off. As father right serves dead fathers, so also does father right serve men whose bodies are dead while their penises are alive.

Against this background, I want to make a simple statement, actually a self-evident observation: *Under father right, the first fact of every human life is that one is birthed by human flesh that belongs to someone barren.* Every human life comes forth from a woman whose body at no moment in her life is not defined as the actual or potential personal property of men. These are the real "facts of life" under father right, the economic realities concerning the labor of mothers. Adult men are entitled to ownership of every body that is birthed and every body that births. Every economic system devised by men—whether capitalism or communism or socialism—is designed to defend male ownership of the bodies and labor of women. Every religious belief system instituted by men—including Judaism, which deifies the father, and Christianity, which deifies the son— is designed to dehumanize the person of the mother. Every psychological system theorized by men—whether the Freudian tradition with its notion of "penis envy" or the modern behaviorist view with its babies in boxes—is designed to validate male ownership of birth itself. Every agency of culture—including the state, the university, medicine, marriage, the nuclear family—is an instrumentality of male ownership of other human lives.

Father right circumscribes how we see, how we feel, and most

---

devastatingly how we imagine. We are so accustomed to definitions of love, justice, and human community that are predicated upon male ownership of other human lives that we can scarcely imagine a future in which people are not property. We are so accustomed to the traumatizing reality that in this civilization the most violent, debilitating, exploitative, and ostensibly intimate relationships between humans are precisely those relations between owner and owned that we cannot imagine being related in any other way. We are so accustomed to imagining that father right merits our respect—because we dare not provoke the father's wrath, because we know in our hearts that he loves only those whom he controls, that he provides if at all only for those lives which he owns, that his approval is bestowed conditionally only upon persons who are his compliant personal property and that he knows no other connection to any other human life—we are so beholden to the father that we have sacrificed and betrayed all mothers in his name.

The Content

In one sense, the origin of father right is inaccessible to our understanding, shrouded in mystery, and lost in the prehistory of civilization. We know male ownership of women's bodies predates written history. We know women were the first slaves and women's bodies were the first capital. We know male ownership of children predates male knowledge of the relationship between coitus and pregnancy. We do not know what mothers knew, for their knowledge has been obliterated. But we know that the first father knew he was a father by virtue of being an owner; he was *paterfamilias*, which literally means "master of slaves." We may suppose that human males invented the power of owning to overshadow the mystery of birthing, and once male ownership was unleashed upon the earth, it knew no bounds, it grew insatiable, and it wanted dominion over all life and death. But we really cannot be certain exactly how lives began to be owned.

In another sense, however, the origin of father right can be understood clearly, for father right reoriginates in generation after generation, quite remarkably regenerating in the lifetime of every male. How does it happen that a human infant, who begins life as the owned property of a father and who is accidentally born with an elongated genital—how does he learn the bizarre propensity to own the lives of other human beings? It is one thing to answer that this society institutionalizes male supremacy and father right and that this society therefore entitles genital males to ownership of female flesh. That's of course true. But it is quite another thing to perceive that in every male lifetime a process is effected, more or less successfully, that produces in the male the character of a father, the behavior of a supremacist, and the capability of owning lives—a capability realized not simply because he is socially entitled to but more profoundly because he is constitutionally dysfunctional otherwise—because, in other words, only owning is erotic. Somehow, every male in his lifetime learns to adjust his entire erotic, emotional, and volitional sensibility in order to become an owner, in contradistinction to women, who are to be owned. Somehow, we must not only abolish the social institutions that sanction father right; we must also discover and analyze the personal origin of father right in every son and begin in this generation to abolish the personal erotic compulsion to own other lives.

In our present culture, there exist mythic renderings of the damage mothers do to sons, wildly inconsistent myths, from the myth of "too much affection" to the myth of "not enough." These myths have enormous power in enforcing the cultural assumption that among the mother's duties to father right is her duty to produce a son who is capable of owning a life like hers. But that is a duty fraught with contradictions. On the one hand, the mother's duty to the father is to remain his carnal possession and to reassure him in his imagination that his son, this little phallic presence, is not a threat to his coital privileges. On the other hand, the mother's duty to the future father in the son is always to present herself as one whom he might like someday to marry—for instance, by reassuring him that unending quantities of her labor are his for the asking. The essential erotic contradiction in all mother-child relationships under father right is described in these words by Alice S. Rossi:

> It is to men's sexual advantage to restrict women's sexual gratification to heterosexual coitus, though the price for the woman and a child may be a less psychologically and physically rewarding relationship.[8]

That erotic contradiction exists whether the child will be raised as a son or a daughter, but if the child grows up a son, the father imagines that the infantile sexuality of his little boy is somehow centered on fucking his wife. Only a father could have imagined that that is what a child wants to do, but that indeed is the fantasy fear of fathers, a fear that requires much coital consolation.

Fathers fantasize all fetuses as male, as repositories of phallic life. This fantasy contradicts not only birth statistics but also the fact of gestation that until the seventh week of fetal development, all fetuses have identical genitalia. This fantasy of fathers, that all fetal life is phallic, only makes sense if it is understood to be an expression of a fundamental characteristic of phallic eroticism: The feelings that become isolated in an adult man's phallus are experienced as disembodied and seem to be left behind in a vagina if his phallus ejaculates and shrinks there. These phallic feelings seem to have been stolen, as accords with his proprietorial world view and his disregard for women, and he imagines that in a fetus those lost phallic feelings are contained and he can somehow have them back. If the baby is born without protuberant external genitalia, the father's projection of phallic life in the fetus stops. But if the baby is born *a boy*, the father's projection of phallic life in the infant continues, and the father perceives the infant as a rival for his wife.

The father's attitudes and actions toward his baby boy are ambivalent at best. The father desired a baby boy in order to retrieve from his wife's body all the erections that disappeared there, to repossess in the form of infant male flesh all the sensations she drained and confiscated from his erect penis. And now what does he do with it? How does he touch it? Or does he not touch it at all? While the father in his ambivalence is waiting for the boy to grow up big and strong, the son is learning the difference between Mother and Not-mother—his first crucial lesson in gender polarity. The child is learning this distinction from information that is tactile, information that is erotic. The child is learning how his own eroticism is in harmony with the eroticism of Mother but in discord with his sensory experience of Not-mother. The child is learning this distinction not on account of anatomy, not on account of lactation in one and the absence of lactation in another. Babies will suckle a male's nipple just as readily as a female's, though few men will permit it. And even babies who were never breast-fed learn the two concepts just as quickly. Rather, the baby is learning the concepts of Mother and Not-mother from a peculiar fact of culture: phallic eroticism in not-mothers is inimical to communion with other human life. Something in Not-mother is alien. Something in Not-mother is dead. Not-mother pats but does not touch. Not-mother fondles but does not feel. Not-mother grabs but does not hold. There is no sensory resonance of pulse and breath and motion between Not-mother and the child. And the child perceives together with the mother that they are different from the not-mother.

By the time this distinction is fixed in the child's consciousness, the father is enraged. From the father's perspective, the child—who is the corporeal projection of his phallic eroticism—is in the clutches of a woman, seemingly subsumed within her body, humiliatingly limp and soft. Now begins the arduous process by which the father will seek again to retrieve from that woman the phallic life that he seems to keep losing. He

---

begins in earnest to repossess his son, for now what is at stake is the father's rather tenuous hold on existence, which seems to stand or collapse with engorgement in his penis and aggression in his son.

The father's struggle to repossess the son will be played out in front of the boy's uncomprehending eyes and upon the bodies of both the boy and the mother. Of course, the father will be aided and abetted by schools, television, and other cultural accessories to the theft of sons from mothers. But the father figure in the flesh will succeed in dividing the boy's eroticism against the mother only by physical or emotional brutality. The boy will be a witness as the father abuses his wife—once or a hundred times, it only needs to happen once, and the boy will be filled with fear and helpless to intercede. Then the father will visit his anger upon the boy himself, uncontrollable rage, wrath that seems to come from nowhere, punishment out of proportion to any infraction of any rules the boy knew existed—once or a hundred times, it only needs to happen once, and the boy will wonder in agony why the mother did not prevent it. From that point onward, the boy's trust in the mother decays, and the son will belong to the father for the rest of his natural life.

It is a pity. The son could have learned from the mother the eroticism of mothering; the son could have learned to feel with, to care for, to cherish other lives. The son could have learned to mother the mother. Instead, the son betrays her.

The authority of the anger of the father is interpreted by the son as follows: (1) Not-mother hates Mother and Not-mother hates me; Not-mother hates us. (2) It is because I am like Mother that Not-mother hates me so. (3) I should be different from Mother; the more different I am from Mother, the safer I will be. These are the cardinal principles of logic in male maturation under father right. They are so simple, even a child can understand. They are backed up by the constant threat of the father's anger, so the child will remember them, and the child will never forget.

The son, in order to become as different from Mother as he can possibly be, now begins to rid his body of the eroticism of the mother. He withdraws from it. He purges it with aggression. He refuses to feel it anymore. In his memory, their sensory identification had been complete. In his whole body, their eroticism had been the same. Now it must be abandoned, negated, canceled, denied; he must no longer feel with her feeling, feel how he feels with her, feel her feeling with him. Every nerve in his body is on guard against her, against continuity with her, against the erotic continuum between them, for fear of the father, who might mistake the son for her. And every nerve in his body is on guard against the father, the father who hates the mother, the father who hates the son who cannot get rid of the mother in his body. All the boy's sensibilities for erotic communion with other life become anesthetized in terror of ever again feeling one with Mother. The boy learns he has a penis and the boy learns the mother does not. If he cannot feel his penis, he will be the same as her for sure. So begins the disembodiment of sensation in that small organ.

Later in his life, the boy's eroticism will inhabit his penis exclusively, the part of him that is not Mother, the one place in his body where he can feel for sure that he is different from her, separate and discrete. He will discover to his frustration that the organ is anatomically incapable of sustaining that obsession. He will not be pleased after ejaculation, when the eroticism in his penis stops, and when he feels a kind of numbness, the death of his phallic life. The more he has purged the memory of the mother from his body, the more and more his phallic eroticism must embody his whole sense of self. This is male identity, defined by the father, defined against the mother. This is male identity, in need of constant verification, in desperate struggle not to identify with the body and eroticism of the mother. The sexual-political content of the relationship of father to son is essentially to divide the son against the mother so that the son will never stop trying to conform to the cultural specifications of phallic identity.

The Consequences and the Conclusion

We live in a two-gender system, in service to the father. There is no justice. There is no peace. That system is inappropriate to the memory of erotic communion with other life.

In fear and in honor of the father, sons learn to deny that memory, to rid their bodies of it. In fear and in honor of the father, sons learn an identity isolated in the phallus.

The father-son relationship is a monument to phallic identity, to the dying of the disembodied penis inside the vagina of a woman. A son must live on to avenge that death. A son must live on to repudiate the mother. A son must be withdrawn from the influence of the mother, which is perceived by the father as dangerous to virility. The son must be terrorized to mistrust her, to stop feeling with her, in order that his identity should reside in his penis. This is an insane inheritance. It is passed on and on and on.

We live in a two-gender system, in service to the father's rage. Sons learn to dissociate, to be immune from the mother. Sons learn the father's rage against the flesh that birthed them, as a condition of escape from the father's condemnation.

That rage is the rage against flesh that is "other"; that rage is the rage against dissolution of self. That rage is the rage of the self that is a fiction, the self that is conditioned in annihilation and denial of another, inherently estranged by cultural definition, identity contingent on nonidentification, the self that must be divided against the mother or it does not exist, it is a nonentity.

Sons can fuck with that rage. Sons can kill with that rage. They can and they do. Still the father is not appeased.

_____

We live in a two-gender system, in service to father right. Fathers, not mothers, invented and control the state. Fathers, not mothers, invented and control the military. Fathers, not mothers, wage war against other peoples. And fathers, not mothers, send sons to war.

Who are the fathers who want sons so much? Who are the fathers and the sons who can only be reconciled in sharing disdain for the life of the mother? And who are the sons who have become fathers to turn sons against mothers again and again?

This servitude must cease. This inheritance must be refused. This system of owning must be destroyed.

Disarmament and Masculinity

A meditation on war

If we could see more clearly
how and why wars are waged, could we see more clearly how to end
them? If we knew more about why men experience combat as the ultimate test of their masculinity, would we know more about how to resolve conflicts in nonviolent ways? If we did not hold on so desperately
to masculinity, might we not also then be able to let go of warfare?

Sons or fathers, poor men or rich men, sacred or secular: all are homosexual in their worship of everything phallic. A sexual revolution might
destroy what men do so well together, away from women: the making
of His-story, the making of war, the triumph of phallic will.
                                                    —Phyllis Chesler

---

A list of sources for the quotations in this essay appears in the Notes, pp. 214–215.

The Politics of Male Sexual Identity

It should require no great imaginative leap to perceive a deep relationship between the mentality of rape and genocide. The socialization of male sexual violence in our culture forms the basis for corporate and military interests to train a vicious military force.

—Mary Daly

The politics of male sexual domination define not only the waging of wars but also the protesting of wars. After the United States military finally got out of Vietnam, this bitter lesson became clear. Women had put their bodies on the line in the movement against that genocidal war. Women had put their bodies on the line alongside young men who were being sent to fight it. But once the war ended, men in the antiwar movement revealed themselves to be completely uninterested in ending *gynocide*, men's eroticized aggression against the gender class women. For these men, rape was merely "a women's issue," whereas ending the war had been "a real radical's issue."

As a woman totally committed to the feminist cause I received several requests ... to march, speak and "bring out my sisters" to antiwar demonstrations "to show women's liberation solidarity with the peace movement," and my response was that if the peace movement cared to raise the issue of rape and prostitution in Vietnam, I would certainly join in. This was met with stony silence on the part of antiwar activists whose catchwords of the day were "anti-imperialism" and "American aggression," and for whom the slogan—it appeared on buttons—"Stop the Rape of Vietnam" meant the defoliation of crops, not the abuse of women.

—Susan Brownmiller

Movement men are generally interested in women occasion⌐''y as bed partners, as domestic-servants–mother-surrogates, and constantly as economic producers: as in other patriarchal societies, one's wealth in the Movement can be measured in terms of the people whose labor one can possess and direct on one's projects.

—Marge Piercy

Disarmament and Masculinity

The fact that wars are waged and rapes are committed by "normal" men—who experience aggression against other life as a paradigm of "manhood"—was entirely ignored by the men who had dominated the antiwar Left. Men ostensibly committed to nonviolence refused even to entertain the notion that war and militarism were functions of male sexual violence—and that male sexual violence is a function of male supremacy. Though they espoused nonviolent, equitable, and nonhierarchical forms of social organization, they continued to act toward women in male-supremacist ways. It became clear that they were interested only in rearrangements of men's power over other men, not in any fundamental change in men's relationships with women. And many women who had been prominent in the movement for peace in Vietnam saw that in giving over their lives to a social-change movement based on terms defined by men, they had been deceived and betrayed.

Pornography is the theory, and rape the practice. And what a practice. The violation of an individual woman is *the* metaphor for man's forcing himself on whole nations (rape as the crux of war), on nonhuman creatures (rape as the lust behind hunting and related carnage), and on the planet itself. . . .

—Robin Morgan

[A]ny commitment to nonviolence which is real, which is authentic, must begin in the recognition of the forms and degrees of violence perpetrated against women by the gender class men.

—Andrea Dworkin

White males are most responsible for the destruction of human life and environment on the planet today. Yet who is controlling the supposed revolution to change all that? White males. . . . It seems obvious that a legitimate revolution must be led by, *made* by those who have been most oppressed: black, brown and white *women*—with men relating to that as best they can.

—Robin Morgan

The Politics of Male Sexual Identity

The post–Vietnam War era reverberated with a betrayal of women by "progressive" men—a betrayal that may be said to be the very essence of whatever political progressivism in this country has ever meant. At no time has an objection to tyranny been couched in terms that even hinted at an objection to men's tyranny over women.

I can not say that I think you very generous to the Ladies, for whilst you are proclaiming peace and good will to Men, Emancipating all Nations, you insist upon retaining an absolute power over wives.
—Abigail Adams to John Adams, 1776

Long before Vietnam, in the movement against slavery in the United States, women, black and white, also put their bodies on the line. But once the slavery of blacks was outlawed, men in the Abolition Movement opposed ending the ownership of women's bodies, black and white, by men—as breeders, as domestic servants, as carnal chattel, and as idiots under the law.

In the abolition movement as in most movements for social change, then as now, women were the committed; women did the work that had to be done; women were the backbone and muscle that supported the whole body. But when women made claims for their own rights, they were dismissed contemptuously, ridiculed, or told that their own struggle was self-indulgent, secondary to the real struggle.
—Andrea Dworkin

It was, again, a bitter lesson. And many women who had been prominent in the movement for abolition saw that they had been deceived and betrayed.

During the late nineteen fifties and early sixties, women put their bodies on the line again in the movement against segregation and racial discrimination. But once the law guaranteed equal rights under the law for black men, men in the Civil Rights Movement opposed the right of women to absolute control over their own bodies and to absolute equality under the law. The right to decide whether and when to birth a child is the bottom line of freedom for women as a class—yet most birth control methods are ineffective and/or harmful and the right to choose abortion is under massive attack. Without the absolute right to true reproductive self-determination, women as a class will continue to be exploited and manipulated in service to the economic, sexual, and psychological priorities of men. In addition, the Equal Rights Amendment has still not passed—over half a century after it was first introduced—and it is in serious danger of not passing ever. Opponents of the ERA are funded by the life insurance industry, which earns billions in profits based directly on women's inequality under the law, and also by various right-wing religious groups. ERA's most powerful opponents perceive accurately that the amendment will force a redistribution of wealth. Yet so-called radical men continued to ignore these issues as "reformist," even as, during the seventies, they established closer and closer economic, ideological, and sexual ties to the pornography industry.

To put it bluntly, feminism is a movement that "radical" men and "the Left" seem only too willing to trash, to ridicule, to put in its "place," or to destroy if *they* can't control it.
                                                    —Gary Mitchell Wandachild

And many women who had been prominent in the movement for civil rights saw that they had been deceived and betrayed.

Now the nuclear-arms race is a clear and present emergency, and in response to that emergency, there has been a growing national and international movement calling for disarmament. But though disarmament now seems as urgent as abolition once did, or as black male civil rights once did, or as peace in Vietnam once did, is there not again deception built into the goals and strategy and political theory of this movement for nuclear disarmament? If our political consciences respond solely to the "doomsday" rhetoric of the nuclear-arms emergency, isn't the betrayal of women again inevitable? Again, we are being told, there is a higher, more pressing cause, one that makes "women's issues" pale by comparison. Thus the threat of nuclear destruction is used by political "progressives" to silence women's demands for civil rights, freedom, and dignity and for an end to sexual violence. And thus the threat of nuclear war is used to manipulate women's guilt in order to maintain the political power of men over women.

"Therefore if you insist upon fighting to protect me, or 'our' country, let it be understood, soberly and rationally between us, that you are fighting to gratify a sex instinct which I cannot share; to procure benefits which I have not shared and probably will not share; but not to gratify my instincts, or to protect myself or my country. For . . . in fact, as a woman, I have no country. . . ."

—Virginia Woolf, *Three Guineas*

During the Vietnam War, for the first time in United States history, young males in large numbers rejected soldiership. Prior to that time, to heed the call of his country and to be a soldier was to be a real man (as the tales of World War II and Korean War veterans still tell us). But during the Vietnam War, a significant cultural adjustment occurred. Large numbers of mothers endorsed their sons' refusal to be cannon fodder. Large numbers of women who were the same age as draftable males identified with those who refused to fight that war. Large numbers of women, across the country, stood by those young males who refused to go to Vietnam and tirelessly labored to bring that war to an end. Large numbers of older men, too—rather than reject those who had rejected military service—admired those young men and encouraged them to resist.

It was very nearly a new moment in the history of men and war: There might then have developed a general consciousness among males that *militarism* is immoral, not simply that particular war in that particular country. There might then have emerged an awareness of the sexual politics of war, the relationship between manhood and violence and the global sex-class system. But that of course was not what happened. Instead, for young males, resistance to military service came to be viewed culturally as being consistent with conventional masculinity: If a young man refused to fight, his power and prerogative in the culture over women was completely intact—in the eyes of himself and in the eyes of enormous numbers of others ("Girls say yes to men who say no" and "Make love not war" were two popular slogans of the time). Thus male resistance to the war in Vietnam became a new and acceptable option for being a real man, instead of an occasion for examining the fundamental relationship between militarism and male supremacy.

Then Abraham lifted up the boy, he walked with him by his side, and his talk was full of comfort and exhortation. But Isaac could not understand him. He climbed Mount Moriah, but Isaac understood him not. Then for an instant he turned away from him, and when Isaac again saw Abraham's face it was changed, his glance was wild, his form was horror. He seized Isaac by the throat, threw him to the ground, and said, "Stupid boy, dost thou then suppose that I am thy father? I am an idolater. Dost thou suppose that this is God's bidding? No, it is my desire."
—Søren Kierkegaard, *Fear and Trembling*

Georg shrank into a corner, as far away from his father as possible. A long time ago he had firmly made up his mind to watch closely every least movement so that he should not be surprised by any indirect attack, a pounce from behind or above.
—Franz Kafka, "The Judgment"

Why, historically, have fathers wanted sons so much—and then why have fathers wanted sons to go to war to be killed?

It is also true that you hardly ever gave me a whipping. But the shouting, the way your face got red, the hasty undoing of the braces and laying

them ready over the back of the chair, all that was almost worse for me.
—Franz Kafka, *Letter to His Father*

In every patriarchal family, there comes a time when the emerging manliness of the son pitches the father into a crisis of ambivalence: This young man is the masculine progeny the father wanted, yet this young man is a youthful physical rival he wanted not at all. Violence is frequently a father's futile attempt to bridge this distance between desire and dread. In the United States, as in other patriarchal nation-states, there exists a class of "superfathers"—the military brass, men who declare and manage wars—who act in other fathers' behalf to keep sons mindful of the power of the father by threatening sons with extinction. It is *boys* who are sent to war. It is aging, adult men who send them. Their mothers and biological fathers may mourn when they die. But the setup—the war machine—keeps father power in place. This is, at root, the psychosexual function of militarism among fathers and sons: The superfathers reinforce a cultural exaggeration of father power over life (progenitation, done by penis) through maintaining the cultural obscenity of father power over death (annihilation, done by weapons—and by sons as extensions of weapons/penises).

When young males refused to fight in Vietnam, they feebly rebelled against male power over their own lives only to ascertain dominance over the lives of women. They did not have the courage and the vision—or perhaps, indeed, the desire—to renounce militarism completely by questioning the institution of patriarchy and by disavowing the cultural power attributed to fathers, in particular fathers' power over sons obtained through the ownership of women's bodies. Instead the sons made a deal—that they would not confront father power head on.

[T]he only way that the Oedipus Complex can make full sense is in terms of power. . . . The male child, in order to save his own hide, has had to abandon and betray his mother and join ranks with her oppressor. He

84

feels guilty. His emotions toward women in general are affected. Most men have made an all-too-beautiful transition into power over others; some are still trying.

—Shulamith Firestone

In war, the fathers castrate the sons by killing them. In war, the fathers overwhelm the penises of the surviving sons by having terrorized them, having tried to drown them in blood.

But this is not enough, for the fathers truly fear the potency of the sons. Knowing fully the torture chambers of male imagination, they see themselves, legs splayed, rectum split, torn, shredded by the saber they have enshrined.

Do it to her, they whisper; do it to her, they command.

—Andrea Dworkin

No woman is ever guaranteed the right to be secure in her own person against forcible violation of her body rights. "Domestic security" within the United States applies only to men; it is a concept that has no real meaning in the lives of women. It does not mean, for instance, freedom for women from male predators who live here—or safety for women even inside their own homes. Unless a woman is visibly in the proprietorship of a male, she is likely to be the victim of heterosexual assault (for example, on any city street). That likelihood is legitimatized by male-supremacist law, custom, and habit, which every normal American man has memorized in his flesh. Many women contract their bodies into marriage for safety (and because, economically, they have no alternative). But the institution of marriage legally sanctions the prerogative of husbands to aggress against their private property, the bodies of their wives.

Each man, knowing his own deep-rooted impulse to savagery, presupposes this same impulse in other men and seeks to protect himself from it. The rituals of male sadism over and against the bodies of women are the means by which male aggression is *socialized* so that a man can associate with other men without the imminent danger of male aggression against his own person.

—Andrea Dworkin

When the superfathers of America speak of "national security," they take for granted that the body rights of men extend to territorial rights and property rights over the bodies of women and children. Defending these body rights is the basis of all relations between groups of men. Under patriarchy, males learn in their own bodies to eroticize aggression—that is, their impulse to act in a way that owns, dominates, and violates another person's body rights has been indelibly conditioned according to a cultural norm of how male eroticism is supposed to feel. Under patriarchy, normally acculturated males assume—correctly—that the same impulse to sexual violence exists in other males. They therefore endeavor to enter into homoerotic truces—nonaggression pacts contracted between men who tacitly agree to aggress against "others" (women, and sometimes weaker men, or men of other races) instead of one another. When a group of men shares power over "their" constituency of women, that sharing assuages their fears of one another's potential for aggression. In their hearts, men grow up terrified of giving offense to, and being attacked by, more violent males. Between men of different nations, armed (phallic) deterrence against forcible violation of the territory they own (the country they own) is men's first line of defense against assault by other men. The military postures of patriarchal nations are modeled exactly on the psychosexual needs of men to defend themselves against personal assault by other men, which can be understood as eroticized violence between males exclusively, and therefore homosexual. When male combat troops do aggress against the territorial rights of other men, their actual military strategy often involves heterosexual rape of the women belonging to those men (for example, American soldiers in Vietnam). But the aggression men fear, and the fear upon which their "national defense" is predicated, is aggression from other men—that is, homosexual attack.

This country's superfathers want to make certain that the United States will have the biggest cock in the world—that is, the greatest potency for sadism, euphemistically referred to as "deterrent" capability—but America faces stiff competition, preeminently from the Soviet Union. Nuclear arms are an extension of men's potency for sadism. Nuclear arms are the capability for the ultimate, masculinity-confirming fuck. That capability fills the imaginations of those who have it and those who don't. As cock power is reckoned, it is in "lethality," the maximum threat that men can imagine wielding against one another. To be perceived as militarily "weak" is by definition to be feminized—vulnerable to attack. To be perceived as having the greatest potency for sadism is, as men imagine, to be "secure"—hence the arms race and the obsession with the quantity bombs prepared to be dropped.

At present, the superfathers of the U.S. and the U.S.S.R. are parties to a precarious, tenuous homoerotic truce whereby the two supercocks:

- endeavor to keep stockpiles of bombs (cock power) balanced;

- agree not to aggress against each other's satellite nations (the male owners of which are themselves in homoerotic alliances with a supercock for protection);

- agree to respect each other's right, within their respective boundaries, to aggress against racial and ethnic minorities; and

- agree to respect any and all national policies prescribing the subjugation of women to men.

The values that inhere on a "small" scale in homoerotic transactions between men are the same values that inhere on a grander scale in all transactions between male-owned and male-supremacist nation-states. The "all-male pack" is essentially contemptuous of anyone who is female or who is construed as feminized, or not really manly. Between all-male packs, their respective commitment to perpetuate violence against women is a token between them of trustworthiness and truce. A male with a greater investment in eroticized aggression can enlist the loyalty of a male with a lesser investment in it simply by offering a promise of "protection" from his sadism. *The arms race cannot be dismantled without dismantling the psychosexual structures of masculinity itself.*

The stated reason for nuclear threat and counterthreat between the supercocks is to preserve and protect the political alignment of satellite nation-states. But the real reason is the need for global allegiance to the existing political alignment of the sexes—and the need for an irrefutable imperative for the maintenance of the sex-class system. Imagine: the superfathers and supercocks of the world locked in nuclear threat and counterthreat as an ultimate deterrent to sex-class rebellion. *To advocate nuclear disarmament without an end to male supremacy is simply to ratify the rights of men and nations to enter into nonaggression pacts among themselves based upon their continued aggression against all women.*

Nothing is more political to a feminist than fucking—nothing is less an act of love and more an act of ownership, violation; nothing is less an instrument of ecstasy and more an instrument of oppression than the penis; nothing is less an expression of love and more an expression of dominance and control than conventional heterosexual relation. Here the war mentality makes a visitation on our bodies and the phallic values of aggression, dominance and conquest are affirmed.

—Andrea Dworkin

As the formula of "fucking as conquest" holds true, the conquest is not only over the female, but over the male's own fears for his masculinity, his courage, his dominance, the test of erection.

—Kate Millett

What is disarmament if it is not the end of male sadism altogether, the end of male eroticized violence, the end of male eroticized aggression? What is disarmament if it is not the end of patriarchy, the end of father right, the end of male supremacy? What do males mean when they say they want disarmament if they have not made a commitment to lay down the dominance they wield over and against women? What, for a male, is nonviolent resistance to the superfathers of patriarchy if it is not repudiating and divesting himself of his birthright to bear arms over and against women's lives?

The Fetus as Penis: Men's Self-interest and Abortion Rights

Men, it is said, do not express their feelings—or if men do, they do so only with great difficulty. Both women and men believe that men are unemotive and unemotional, that inside men's tender psyches is a wellspring of feelings, stonewalled and speechless. Men respect and fear other men whose feelings are undisclosed and well defended. Women also respect and fear such men whose feelings lie dormant beneath a permafrost of mastery. And women who live with them implore them privately to emote just a little, begging them to say what they are feeling, begging them to warm. But men do not express their feelings. Or so the story goes.

In fact, throughout history, men as a class have always expressed their feelings, eloquently and extensively: Men have expressed their feelings about women, death, and absent fathers and turned those feelings into religions. Men have expressed their feelings about women, wealth, possession, and territory and turned those feelings into laws and nation-states. Men have expressed their feelings about women, murder, and the masculinity of other men and from those feelings forged battalions and detonable devices. Men have expressed their feelings about women, fucking, and female rage against subjection and formed those feelings into psychiatry. Men have *institutionalized* their feelings, so that whether or not a particular man is feeling the feeling at a particular time, the feeling is being expressed through the institutions men have made.

Today, men's feelings about women's increasing refusal to shore up men's delusions of grandeur are being expressed in a bitter battle to keep women's reproductive capacities within male control. The dimensions of this battle are staggering.* According to a nationwide study conducted by the National Center for Health Statistics, one fifth of all babies born in the United States—or a total of 14 million people—would not have been born if their mothers had given birth only to those babies they wanted at the time they got pregnant.[1] Currently, more than half a million women each year want to have an abortion but cannot get one because the service is not available, so they have no choice but to birth a child.[2]

The warfare against reproductive self-determination for women is being waged both overtly and covertly. In its overt form, poor women are denied abortions because they cannot afford them;[3] eight out of ten public hospitals refuse to perform the abortion procedure;[4] federal and drug-company funding for contraception research has plummeted;[5] and a growing right-wing/fundamentalist coalition has mobilized to write embryos and zygotes into the Constitution (through a so-called human-life amendment stating that "life begins at the moment of conception," which would make abortion a crime and millions of women murderers)—and to keep women written out (by stopping ratification of the Equal Rights Amendment). The war is being waged covertly in the form

---

* The statistics that follow reflect the time when I first gave this speech in 1978. The situation in 1988 is no better, and in many ways worse.

of men's apathy and passivity in relation to contraception, men's private pressures on women to carry to term pregnancies that the women did not want, and the resistance of men who claim they endorse abortion rights to make women's right to choose a priority in their political activism.

The women forced to bear unwanted children are the POWs in this war. For most of them, after nine months of labor, their incarceration inside a diminished life has just begun.

What are the statistical chances that a woman will need and get an abortion? And what are the chances that a man will be involved in a conception that is aborted? What, in other words, is the *risk rate* over a woman's lifetime, and what is the *responsibility rate* over a man's? Given the current frequency of abortions in the United States, it can be predicted that over the course of all American women's lifetimes, two out of three will have an abortion. And the rate of involvement for men is the same: Over the course of their lifetimes, two out of three men will have been responsible for impregnating a woman who subsequently decides to abort.[6]

The trend is that more and more women are deciding to terminate the pregnancies they do not want. Year by year, the number of elective abortions has gone up by about 15 percent. This year, over a million were performed, legally and safely—approximately one abortion for every three live births.[7]

But there is also a trend toward increasingly repressive and restrictive laws, increasing harassment and violence against abortion clinics, and an increasingly antipathetic medical establishment. For example, ordinances are being enacted on the city level across the country to require abortion patients to be shown pictures of fetal development and to be told they might have emotional problems if they go through with an abortion. In some places, the fact that a woman has had an abortion can be used against her in a child-custody trial as evidence that she is an unfit mother. In eight out of ten counties, mostly rural areas, there is not a single doctor or clinic that will provide the abortion procedure.[8]

These two trends are on a collision course. And seething beneath the surface of this crisis is a mass of male feeling—resentful and punitive—now being institutionalized before our very eyes. Men's individual feelings are diverse and complex, but they can be understood as having in common the fear that women will cease to sustain the sexual identities of men, and the fear that therefore masculinity will cease to exist.

One of the few surveys of men's attitudes toward abortion was conducted in Philadelphia—a few years before the 1973 Supreme Court decision legalizing abortion—among 424 men who were heads of families, mostly men who were living with their wives and children. These men were asked the question "Do you favor or oppose abortion?" under six hypothetical circumstances in which a woman might consider terminating a pregnancy.

• In the case of *financial hardship* where it would not be possible to support an additional child, three out of four of these men opposed abortion.

• In the case of a pregnancy that would result in *a child not wanted*, four out of five of these men opposed abortion.

• In the case of a pregnancy that was due to a *failure in birth control method* being used, five out of six of these men opposed abortion.

These men's feelings became clear: The only situations in which a majority would favor abortion involved cases of a wife's bad health, a wife raped, or the possibility of a deformed child [9]—in other words: spoiled goods.

Men's indifference to learning about contraception and to taking any responsibility for it is a theme that emerges from many reports of projects that have attempted, and failed, to reach and educate men. One of the most successful programs of contraception education for men, a Planned Parenthood project in Chicago, abandoned its attempts to reach men over the age of twenty-five when it was found that these men simply would not participate, even when offered beer, sandwiches, free condoms—and "stag" movies.[10] Instead, the project targeted a younger group, and as part of its research the project conducted a survey of over a thousand men aged fifteen to nineteen:

- These young men were asked whether they agreed with the statement "It's okay to tell a girl you love her so that you can have sex with her." Seven out of ten agreed that it's okay.
- They were asked whether they agreed with the statement "A guy should use birth control whenever possible." Eight out of ten disagreed and said a guy should not.
- And when asked, "If I got a girl pregnant, I would want her to have an abortion," nearly nine out of ten said no, they would not want her to have an abortion.

These teenage men agreed: Deception to obtain coital access is okay; male irresponsibility in contraception is okay; but abortion is not okay—"because it's wrong."[11]

Largely because of attitudes such as these, one million teenage women—one tenth of all teenage women—become pregnant each year, and two thirds of their pregnancies are not wanted.[12]

The one-to-one reality is that men exert an overwhelming influence over the contraceptive practices and childbearing choices of women. Nearly all men, in their day-to-day lives, control the fertility of the women closest to them in the same way they control other aspects of women's lives: by establishing the boundaries within which she is "safe" from his anger, which is backed up by force. Knowing that he can make her life miserable if she transgresses, if she crosses him in any way, she opts for a lesser misery. As she surrenders her will to his, it doesn't make a lot of difference whether she does so grudgingly, thinking, "He's making me do this," or whether she does so completely browbeaten, believing, "This is what I wanted to do anyway." What matters is that *he* gets his way. Often as not, she carries an unwanted pregnancy to term rather than provoke her male partner's threatening rage. It's easier, she imagines, to live with the screaming of a defenseless, unwanted child.

The Politics of Male Sexual Identity

On the postpartum floor of a large New York City hospital, Dr. Maria Boria-Berna interviewed 130 women who had just given birth and approximately 100 men who had impregnated them. She asked the men how they felt about their wife's using birth control. The majority of the men "did not like the idea at all." She asked the women how they felt about using birth control, and eight out of ten replied that they "favored contraception without reservation." But about half of the women favoring contraception said that if their husband objected, they would defer and not use any. At that rate of deference to the determined will of husbands, it is not surprising that 48 percent of these new mothers reported that their pregnancy had been totally unplanned.[13]

Men as a class are devoted to the sex act that deposits their semen in a vagina—"in situ" as men have so tellingly named their target. And men as a class are firmly attached to the idea that any issue resulting is proof positive they are manly.

Men control women's reproductive capacities in part because men believe that fetuses are phallic—that the ejaculated leavings swelling up in utero are a symbolic and material extension of the precious penis itself. This belief is both literal and metaphoric, both ancient and modern. The mythology of the fetus as a purely male substance harbored inside the body of a nonmale host reaches back at least as far as fifth century B.C. Greece. In a classic statement of it, the tragedian Aeschylus has the male god Apollo declare:

The mother is no parent of that which is called her child, but only nurse of the new-planted seed that grows. The parent is he who mounts. A stranger she preserves a stranger's seed . . . [14]

Down through the ages, ranks of theologians and other influential male thinkers have ratified this view. (And in at least one language, Old High German, the words for "penis" and "fetus" are related and nearly identical—*faselt* and *fasel.*) Freud, for instance, probably speaking for many men, projected onto women his feelings about fetuses this way:

The wish with which the girl turns to her father is no doubt originally the wish for the penis which her mother has refused her and which she now expects from her father. The feminine situation is only established, however, if the wish for a penis is replaced by one for a baby, if, that is, a baby takes the place of a penis in accordance with an ancient symbolic equivalence. . . . Her happiness is great if later on this wish for a baby finds fulfillment in reality, and quite especially so if the baby is a little boy who brings the longed-for penis with him.[15]

The modern version of the mythology of the fetus as a penis is the notion that the fetus is a person. This notion makes perfect sense if one realizes that personhood itself is phallic by cultural definition: In this male-supremacist culture, authentic personhood accrues to men and not to women because men have a penis and women do not. To say that the fetus is a person is to say that its civil rights supersede those of its host (who is *not* male and therefore *not* fully a person), which is another way of saying that fetal matter has worth that only penile tissue can bestow. By contrast, women's actual lives hardly count at all. As Andrea Dworkin describes it,

The womb is dignified only when it is the repository of holy goods—the phallus or, since men want sons, the fetal son. To abort a fetus, in masculinist terms, is to commit an act of violence against the phallus itself. It is akin to chopping off a cock. Because a fetus is perceived of as having a phallic character, its so-called life is valued very highly, while the woman's actual life is worthless and invisible since she can make no claim to phallic potentiality.[16]

The history of men's ideas is the history of what men feel and the history of what men feel to be real. As a class, men never feel more real than when their penises are erect and penetrating—and never feel less real than when their penises are flaccid. As a result, men's ideas about what is real, what is objectively as real as themselves, tend to be utterly self-referential and almost entirely phallocentric. Rarely does a man's empathy extend beyond what he believes can be felt by other men, because if *men* do not feel something, the feeling is literally not real. The war against reproductive self-determination for women is a war to defend the reality of phallic power. In this phallocentric culture, a woman's unwillingness to admit a man's "manhood" and accept his proffered "seed"—or a woman's unwillingness to incubate the stuff—is felt at some level to be an act of violence against men's personhood. Since phallic personhood is contingent on female deference, nurturance, and sustenance all its life in order to differentiate and thrive, any female noncooperation—whether in fucking or breeding—is perceived as an attack on men's core selves.

Many women decide to have an abortion and do not tell their male partner anything about it. This was the decision of 15 percent of the women in one group of abortion patients interviewed at a clinic in New York City.[17] Some women decide to have an abortion, make an appointment, then change their minds and carry to term. A group of such women in New Haven were asked six months later what had made them change their minds. The reason given most often was "religious and moral objections." The reason given second most often was that their partner desired a baby.[18]

Still other women decide to abort; but because they are confronted in their personal lives with a conspicuous lack of support for their decision from their male partner, their abortion experience is particularly stressful. It is often alleged that abortion is in and of itself an emotionally devastating experience for women; antiabortion agitators frequently warn women of its psychic perils. But a quite different picture emerges from a study among 329 abortion patients in Philadelphia. While it was true that "most women experienced their abortions with some degree of conflicting emotions," the majority reported their predominant feeling was "relief that the abortion had been performed." Significantly, this study isolated the critical effect of men's attitudes on how women felt about their abortion experience. According to the researcher, Ellen Freeman, of the University of Pennsylvania School of Medicine,

---

Frequently, women were more concerned about their relationships with their male partners than with any other aspect of the abortion. They needed and tried to include their partners in the experience. In almost all instances in which respondents experienced substantial emotional distress, it was because they lacked emotional support from their partners.[19]

There are, as of course there always are, exceptions—men of good intentions, men actively and wholeheartedly attempting to give women support through their abortion experience. When 171 abortion patients were interviewed at one New York City clinic, half of them said their male partner wholeheartedly supported the decision to have an abortion.[20] At another typical urban clinic, it was found that men accompanied about one out of ten of the women who arrived to have an abortion. A majority of those men, when asked, expressed a strong desire to be there, a strong feeling that "they should participate directly in preventing unwanted pregnancies," and the belief that both partners are responsible for the decision to have an abortion. Nevertheless, these men were found to be generally ignorant about the type and safety of the medical procedure that their partner had come there to have. And fully eight out of ten reported that the current unwanted pregnancy occurred because no contraception had been used—and the reason they gave most often was "carelessness."[21]

Why does reproductive self-determination for women so terrify men, threaten men, anger men? It is as if in some primal, private part, men dread that if their mother really had a choice, they might not have been born to begin with. And it is as if men—who on the whole age very badly, increasingly obsessed with penile tumescence, increasingly estranged from any other life, from any other flesh—also dread this: that if women truly had a choice, men's sons would not be born.

I believe that men as a class know that reproductive freedom for women is not in men's interest. Men know this in their guts. Men as a class know that if reproductive freedom for women ever became a reality, male supremacy could no longer exist. It's as simple and logical as that;

and men's laws, men's dollars, and men's gods serve that knowledge. Men as a class know that their social and cultural and economic advantage over and against women depends absolutely upon the continuance of involuntary pregnancy, involuntary gestation, involuntary parturition, and involuntary child rearing. Men know that the very continuity of their gender class—the continuity of "masculinity" as a distinct and imperious gender identity and the continuity of "men" as a distinct and imperious power bloc—requires that everyone born without a penis live her whole life palpably circumscribed and controlled by the will of anyone born *with* a penis. Otherwise, the penis would lose its social meaning as the fundamental determinant of all secular and sacred power. When that happens—when the mere fact of a penis no longer entitles anyone on earth to unjust power over anyone else's life—then, in effect, men will no longer exist.

I dare to say I want that future to happen.

What Is "Good Sex"?

I
What is the relationship between the way a man has sex and the way he acts the rest of the time?

The question assumes that there *is* a relationship—and that a man's erotic life and behavior have some connection to the ethics of all his acts, all the choices of action that he makes, all the values expressed by all of his behavior. The question assumes that how a man acts in sex and how he acts in general are not separate spheres, but perhaps rather a unity, perhaps a continuum, perhaps fundamentally the same problem. The question assumes that each man has a character—a way he characteristically makes choices having ethical meaning—and the question assumes that his singular character is expressed and can be observed both in and out of explicitly sexual contexts.

Needless to say, this is not a popular way to think about the way most men have sex—or the way most men live their lives. According to the vastly more common view, the values a man expresses in the way he has sex are in fact circumscribed by the sexual context and isolated there, such that "whatever happens there happens *there*." This more common view has it that sex is sex and the rest is the rest. A great deal of sexual shame both originates in this view and is neatly obscured by this view. Think, for instance, of the shame and panic in a man who is touching another man in affection for the first time when up to that point, in the rest of his life, he had acted as if the values in that touch were loathsome. Think, simultaneously, of the insular and insolent ease with which a man can privately manhandle or humiliate or injure someone else for his sexual gratification, then just go on with his life as if the meanings of what he had done and the fact that he had done it stopped at the torture chamber door—indeed as if the meaning of whatever happens in private between two consenting adults is not only nobody else's business; it's not even the business of the people who did it. Great quantities of various substances get ingested in order to erect a barricade around the sexual arena secure enough to support this view, secure enough to blockade memory, secure enough to obliterate shame. It's called releasing inhibitions. What it means is getting wrecked enough to be able to believe that what happens in sex is separate. A great deal goes on between people in sex that remains incomprehensible— sometimes suffocatingly and woundingly inaccessible to later reflection and integration— because of this notion that how a man acts in sex is unrelated to how he acts all the rest of the time (and anyway, "Who do you think you are questioning what happened between us last night? We had great sex, didn't we?"). Such repression of so many raw feelings, so many contradictory, unsorted-out emotions; so much repression of consciousness—

this is believed to be liberating; this is believed to be freedom; this is believed to facilitate and culminate in the having of good sex.

II
What is good sex?

And what kind of a question is that? I suggest, first of all, that it is a philosophical question in the classical sense: an important question, a profound question, maybe even an unanswerable question, but a question that nevertheless demands we meet it with all our powers of imagination and comprehension. Classically, the question could be one of either aesthetics or ethics: Is good sex good because it is aesthetically satisfying—beautiful and pleasing to the senses? or is good sex good ethically, because of the ethical values in the way the partners act toward each other, how they treat each other—perhaps the justice and equality between them and their empathy and respect for each other's bodily integrity? In my own experience, good sex has both an aesthetic and an ethical aspect: The erotic pleasure deepens in and depends on a context of acting that is mutually respecting, mutually good for and good toward each other; while at the same time the sensory exchange of physical pleasure expresses an ethic in the relationship's history that is mutually valued because it is considerate and just. In my own view, when you ask the question "What is good sex?" philosophically, you are in effect asking two questions merged as one: You are asking about the relationship in sex between pleasurable sensation and principled action.

When you ask the question "What is good sex?" you are also asking, I suggest, a question that is profoundly political, because its answer requires an inquiry into structures of power disparity between people— political structures based primarily on gender and also on race, money, and age. Is sex perceived to be good ultimately with reference to those categories?—for instance, does a man perceive sex to be good because he experiences it as enhancing his hold on the status of his gender; through the act of fucking, for instance, does he feel politically empowered, sensorially attached to his membership in a superior sex caste; does he therefore perceive fucking per se as good sex? Or is sex good to the extent that it transcends power inequities—to the extent that sex between two individuals mitigates the power disparity that they bring with them from the social context? In theory, two people might approach a particular sexual encounter either as a ritual celebration of the social power differences between people in general and between them in particular or as a personal act of *repudiating* all such power inequities. Someone whose sexuality has become committed to celebrating the political status quo would consider sex good to the extent that its scenario achieves actual and lasting physical sensations of power inequity— through dominance, coercion, force, sadomasochism, and so forth. But someone who chose actively to resist the political status quo would consider sex good to the extent that it empowers both partners equally— and to the extent that they succeed together in keeping their intimacy untainted by the cultural context of sexualized inequality. The political question is tough, but it's important to remember that it *is* a political question, and that "What is good sex?" is a question about the relationship between the social structure and the particular sex act.

So-called sexual liberation has not provided a conceptual vocabulary that is very useful for discerning whatever is good about good sex either philosophically or politically. There is a lot of mindless jargon in the air (" 'Sex positive' " is good; 'sex negative' is bad." "Prosex—any kind of sex—is good; antisex is very bad") combined with a kind of sexual-orientation chauvinism ("All gay sex is good; no gay sex is bad" or, as the case may be, "All straight sex is good; no straight sex is bad") that results in a near-total obfuscation of the actual values in particular sexual encounters. In the so-called sexual-liberationist frame of reference, the question "What is good sex?" gets answered pretty quantitatively—in terms of erections, orifices, ejaculations, orgasms, hunkiness, hotness—and in terms of how far the anatomical experience can be removed from any context of social meaning. In the sexual-liberationist frame of reference, any other notion of good sex is caricatured as "goody-goody," "correct," "puritan," "vanilla." This frame of reference is derived from the belief that laws, parents, the church and the state, and women in general were all forces of repression keeping men from having as many outlets as they pleased for their so-called sexual tension. But today there is no way to ask the question "What is good sex?" merely in terms of sexual-liberationist rhetoric. Today the question must be asked looking at a social structure that is essentially male supremacist and looking at the function of sexual behavior in that structure—at how sexual action in private can reflect and keep intact larger social structures of dominance and submission, at how hatred of "the other" can be sexualized until it no longer feels like hate because it feels so much like sex. And there is no way anymore that anyone can answer the question "What is good sex?" without in some sense expressing either a reactionary or a revolutionary political position—an opinion, a point of view, about the male supremacy of the social order: whether it should stay the same . . . or whether it should not.

III
Which sex is sex "better" with?

Ultimately it is not possible to support one's belief in gender polarity (or "sex difference") without maintaining gender hierarchy (which in our culture is male supremacy). Clinging to "sex difference" *is* clinging to male supremacy. And our "sexual orientation" is one of the ways we've learned to cling.

To be "oriented" toward a particular sex as the object of one's sexual expressivity means, in effect, having a sexuality that is like target practice—keeping it aimed at bodies who display a particular sexual definition above all else, picking out which one to want, which one to get, which one to have. Self-consciousness about one's "sexual orientation" keeps the issue of gender central at precisely the moment in human experience when gender really needs to become profoundly peripheral. Insistence on having a sexual orientation in sex is about defending the status quo, maintaining sex differences and the sexual hierarchy; whereas *resistance* to sexual-orientation regimentation is more about where we need to be going.

The sensuality that may be occasioned by intimacy, trust, and fairness is quite unlike that sexuality which is driven to hit on a particular gender embodiment. The sensuality that arises in a relational context of actual people being together and actually being themselves—not stand-ins for a gender type—is radically different from that sexuality which requires that the "other" not deviate from a particular standard of sexedness. Such a sensuality may be deeply satisfied with giving expression and meeting a mutually felt responsiveness. It may not necessarily be driven to culminate in any particular anatomical completion. The resolution it seeks may simply be the offered and received and thoroughly responded-to expression, which may be experienced in a particular relational context as a transient release from gender altogether. (This sensual possibility is what explains why someone who has an ostensible sexual orientation may nevertheless, in a particular relationship, be quite sexually expressive and responsive with someone who is not apparently the "object" of that orientation. This sensual possibility may also occur between people who might seem to be one another's "appropriate" gender choice but who—despite that—have actually come together as whole individuals with a particular relational history, not as emblems of a gender.)

IV
What is the relationship between good sex and commercial representations of sex?

Explicit representations of sex in commercial films and videos reflect and influence what many men imagine and perceive to be "good sex." Seen on the screen, the sex in sex films epitomizes the kinds of sex, and the values in that sex, that men as a class (or at least as a consumer market) aspire to. To view sex acts through the medium and technology of film or video is therefore like looking through a window at what millions and millions of men believe is the best sex there is: sex that purports to be good—or "great," as the case may be.

Gay male sex films offer a particularly focused view of what men believe that *other* men experience when they're having good sex. Of course gay male sex films do not necessarily offer a paradigm of good *sex object*—most men would in fact probably find gay sex films repellent on that score. But however distasteful gay male sex films might be to men who do not participate in the gender-specific objectification and fetishism for which the films are intended, the films themselves reveal a great deal about the relationship between a male viewer and the idealized male sexual subject—the one who is shown in the throes of presumably good (for him) sex. Like almost all sex films, gay male sex films represent sex that has no past (the couplings are historyless), no future (the relationships are commitmentless), and virtually no present (it is physically functional but emotionally alienated). In a real sense, gay male sex films cross over the "sexual orientation" line because they epitomize those qualities of voyeurism and self-involvement in sex that straight men also aspire to.

Gay male sex films typically comprise explicit sex scenes, frequently between strangers, often with a sound track consisting solely of music and dubbed-in groans. During these sex scenes there is almost always an erect penis filling the screen. If the camera cuts away from the penis, the

---

107

camera will be back within ten seconds. Scenes are set up so that closeups of penises and what they are doing and what is happening to them show off to best advantage. Most of the closeups of penises are of penises fucking in and out of asses and mouths, being blown, or being jacked off.* A penis that is not erect, not being pumped up, not in action, just there feeling pretty good, is rarely to be seen: you wouldn't know it was feeling if it wasn't in action; and in the world of gay male sex films, penises do not otherwise feel anything.

Curiously, there is a great deal of repression of affect in gay male sex films—a studied impassivity that goes beyond amateur acting. The blankness of the faces in what is ostensibly the fever pitch of passion suggests an unrelatedness not only between partners but also within each partner's own body. This is sex labor that is alienated, these dead faces seem to say.

The film edits go by quickly. A few seconds at one angle. Then a few seconds over there. The camera on the cock. Almost always on the cock. The cock almost always hard and pumping. No moments in between anything. How did they get from that to this? Quick cut to the cock. Wait, in between there, wasn't there a moment between them when they just briefly—? Cut. Cut. The rhythms of the sex film are the staccatos of sexual disconnecting; they are not the rhythms of any credible sequence of sexual communion—those moments of changing pace, touching base, remembering who you're with, expressing, responding. All of that is cut out. All of that doesn't show. All that shows is "the action": the progress of the cock, the status of the cock. (You know when you're having sex with a man who learned how from watching sex films: no transitions.)

---

* At the time I wrote this, late 1982, no gay male sex films had been produced that took into account what was to emerge as the AIDS crisis. Although I have made extensive revisions in my original text, I haven't changed its "pre-AIDS" frame of reference in my descriptions of filmed sex acts, because the gay male sex film market is still today much the same.

What Is "Good Sex"?

Most of the sex acts are acts of detaching. In typical sucking shots, for instance, there the two men are, with a blow job going on between them, and they might as well be at a glory hole. The sex acts in gay sex films have the illusion of forging a connection, in the sense of hooking up plumbing; but they seem to be experienced as acts of abstracting-apart, of getting off by going away someplace, of not being there with any-body. (Which reminds me I once asked a gay male friend what was the greatest number of people he had ever had sex with at one time. His answer: "Five-eighths.")

The sex that is had in gay male sex films is the sex that is showable. And what is shown about it is the fetishized penis. When the obligatory cum shot comes, you see it in slow motion, perhaps photographed from several angles simultaneously, the penis pulled out of its orifice just for the occasion, being pumped away at, squirting, maybe someone trying to catch it in his mouth. There's no way to show how orgasm feels, and the difference between the reality and the representation is nowhere more striking than in the cum shot—a disembodied spurt of fluid to certify the sex is "real."

All that is shown in gay male sex films is presented as conspicuously *male*, of course; imputations about optimum *female* sexual functioning are lacking. Heterosexual pornography constructs a mythology about female will and desire, always showing the woman as sex object with an insatiable craving for subordination. Much less cinematic attention is paid to the male sexual subject—for two reasons, presumably: (1) The straight male viewer wants to imagine *himself* in the sex scenes and he does not particularly care to be distracted by the phallic competition and (2) the straight male viewer prefers not to be unnerved by his own potential to sexually objectify other men's bodies. Hence, the emphasis in heterosex-ual pornography is the female as object—and her slavish lust for what-ever men want to do to her to put her down—so that the male viewer can project himself onto her debased body and get off.

Gay male sex films characteristically depict the male body as sex

---

object, but insofar as they also display the male body functioning prominently as sexual subject, gay male sex films present a distillation of what nearly all men believe enviable sex in an anatomically male body might be like if they were ever to have endless quantities of it themselves. As artifacts of a heterosexist culture that is rigidly polarized by gender, gay male sex films exhibit the apotheosis of male sexual functioning as imagined by men who, not unlike straight men, dread the taint of feminization.

So what exactly are we being told in gay male sex films about the way male bodies ought to subjectively experience sex? Even leaving aside the rough stuff of gay male pornography—the scenes of forced fellatio, assault and molestation, humiliation and exploitation, chaining and bondage, the violence often interlarded among the allegedly noncoercive sucking and fucking as if to tip us off that in all this sex we are seeing there really is an undercurrent of force and domination—even leaving aside all of that, what exactly is there in the merely explicit sex scenes that recommends itself as good sex? What are we being told that sex can mean *between* people, if anything? What are we being told about what men must become in order to have what looks like blockbuster sex? What are we being told to do with the rest of ourselves?—what are we being told to lop off from ourselves and the history of our relationships with one another and our responsibilities to one another in order to feel at liberty to have sex at all?

The values in the sex that is depicted in gay male sex films are very much the values in the sex that gay men tend to have; they are very much the values in the sex that straight men tend to have; they are very much the values that male supremacists tend to have: taking, using, estranging, dominating—essentially, sexual powermongering.

Many men consume sex films and videos because watching these media makes them feel like having sex when they don't particularly feel like having sex—and men *don't like* the feeling of not feeling like having sex. There's a fairly common compulsion among men to feel they should feel like having sex even when they don't. It's as if men don't really feel their male identity unless they're experiencing their own body in a way that is explicitly, culturally, sexually phallic. Commercial representations of sex help men over those unpleasant little hurdles when their sexual apparatus is not especially raring to go. Such media help men feel real more of the time by helping men feel like wanting to have sex more often. In combination with drugs, which in various ways induce a heightened sense of sexedness, commercial representations of sex prop up men's sexual identities and keep men in touch with an ideal of solipsistic masculinity—quite out of touch with anyone else.

Moreover, many men tend to have the kind of sex that people having sex for a camera tend to have. Men learn from sex films how to have the kind of sex that is observable from without, not necessarily experienceable from within. "Showable" and "performable" sex is not particularly conducive to communicating what is going on emotionally between two people in sex, the values in it, how this sexual encounter is related to the rest of their lives, and so forth. The physical expressions and sensations that carry this kind of information between people do not photograph well, if at all. What a camera can see is not remotely equivalent to what a person can express and perceive with another person during sex. But if what a camera can see becomes a man's operational standard for "good sex"—if a man models his sexual behavior after that which is displayable on a screen and if, in addition, *he becomes like a camera* in relation to the person he is with—then a crucial potential for erotic communication has been occluded. Many men experience the values in explicit sex films as synonymous with the values they most desire in their own sex life because the medium's form and content—voyeurism, detachment, objectification, absence of inner emotional continuity and sensation—are congruent with their own habituated sexuality. Once a man's ideal of sexual experience has been mediated by photographic technology, he may become unable to experience sex other than as a machinelike voyeur who spasms now and then. And since the relation of voyeur to viewed is implicitly a power imbalance, such a man may become unable to perceive "good sex" where there is no implied domination.

V
How can anyone ever learn what good sex really is if they haven't ever had it?

At this point, aficionados of pornography will perhaps protest: But sex films are still emerging as a communications medium and they have yet to reach their full, "artistic" potential. So of course the sex films need to be improved, with enhanced production values, more believable story lines, upgraded acting . . . you know . . . better lighting. The solution, some will say, is to change the way that sex films are made.

Frankly, I don't think that will do. The solution, I believe, is really to change the way that sex is had. Here's what I mean:

Let's assume that there exists an authentic erotic potential between humans such that mutuality, reciprocity, fairness, deep communion and affection, total body integrity for both partners, and equal capacity for choice-making and decision-making are merged with robust physical pleasure, intense sensation, and brimming-over expressiveness. Let's say that some people have actually already experienced that erotic potential and some people have never. Let's say, further, that the experience of this erotic potential occurred quite against the odds—because given the prevailing social values about sex, it could not have been predicted that two people would ever find out that this erotic potential exists. Everything about the cultural context would seem to predict that sexual meetings would be tainted with or steeped in shame and guilt, hierarchy and domination, contempt and repulsion, objectification and alienation, sexually crippling incidents from childhood, or simply emotional absence from each other. But as luck would have it, a few folks happen upon an erotic potential that is actually rooted in the same values that bring kindness and exuberance and intimacy to the rest of their life. So then the question becomes: How does anyone pass along their knowledge of that potential to other folks on the planet—how do they express it, show it, *communicate* it—without having to sleep with everyone?

Some cultural artifacts will of course be necessary to get the word out—to attempt to convey to people what can be good about sex and to help people disentangle their sexual histories from the social norms that keep sex from being good. There will need to be expressions in the form of many kinds of messages—words, pictures, performances, combinations. Information will need to be shared, but I imagine that this communication would be very different from most sexually explicit media that now exist, which are essentially things made for consumers to have a sexual relationship to. The whole point of communicating about this human erotic possibility is that people be whole people to one another—not parts, not things, not objects, not consumables. Obviously, then, the media appropriate to such communication cannot itself be produced and marketed as things to have sex with—as "orgasm totems"—which would merely reinforce sexual relating to *people* as things.

But the human connection has to begin among us. The human communication cannot wait to be mediated.

What I believe needs to happen is a radical reexamination of the values in the kinds of sex we are having. We need to make a commitment to responsibility and responsiveness in sex. We need to make a personal commitment to stay conscious during sex, to stay alert to what is going on even as it is going on, a commitment to being ethically awake instead of doped. As individuals, and perhaps as friends (I don't believe there is any readiness for this in any existing movement), we need to begin to understand more about what is going on between us when we have sex, the values in it, how it is related to the rest of our lives, how it is related to how we treat people, and how it is related to political change—and we need to talk about it all, face to face, one to one, before, during, and after.

Our bodies have learned many lies. If we dare to be ruthlessly honest, we can perhaps recover truth.

Part III

Pornography and Male Supremacy

The Forbidden Language
of Sex

For a panel on pornography, at a writers' congress

The language of sex that is
forbidden used to be language like this:

Cal's huge, lust-bloated member sliced viciously into her hotly clasping
pussy, and every time his hot swollen balls slapped against her ass she
let out a deep groan of unbearable pleasure.[1]

The language of sex that is forbidden used to be language like this:

"Bitch," he snapped, pulling away from her, yanking his dick out of her
mouth. "You're trying to make me come before I'm ready. You know I
like to fuck your ass before I come! You inconsiderate bitch!" he spat,
knowing how she ate up that kind of talk.[2]

The language of sex that is forbidden used to be language like this:

"Take it, you cunt, take your punishment," he growled, whirling the whip around his head and cracking it down against my buttocks. "You take your punishment, bitch, you take all of it, you slut!"

The whip lashed into my thighs and I screamed in the exquisite grip of agony as it burned me with a wonderful almost fire-like passion. He cracked the vicious tool against my legs another time, laughing almost wildly with every blow. . . .

"Ohh, God, Martin, yes, yes," I wailed, twisting and turning to meet his attack. "Again, Martin, hit me again! I love it, I need it, harder, harder, harder!"

He tore into me even more viciously than before. . . .

He was beside himself with pleasure now, just raining the blows down upon me with a cruel, vicious delight. He didn't care about anything then, expect [sic] the screams that tore from my lips and echoed, delightfully, in his ears.

"Ahh, yeah, bitch, take it, take my discipline," he growled, crashing the whip into me over and over again. "I know you love it, cunt, I know you do!" [3]

The language of sex that is forbidden used to be language like this:

"Shut up, you bitch you!" I said. "It hurts does it? You wanted it, didn't you?" I held her tightly, raised myself a little higher to get it into the hilt, and pushed until I thought her womb would give way. Then I came—right into that snail-like mouth which was wide open. She went into a convulsion, delirious with joy and pain. Then her legs slid off my shoulders and fell to the floor with a thud. She lay there like a dead one, completely fucked out. [4]

Not long ago, language like that was the language of political radicalism: it gave offense to entrenched powers, it was dangerous, it sought to overthrow an oppressive system of sexual repression, and so it had to be stopped. The struggle over the permissibility of such language was waged among factions of men—men publishers, men legislators, men jurists, men lawyers—for the rights of men writers and men readers to produce and consume it, wherever and whenever they wanted.

Today the language of sex that is forbidden has changed. Today's forbidden language of sex gives offense to the sexual egos of men as a gender class. It challenges the force and objectification and contempt and violence in male sexual behavior and identifies that behavior as the root and paradigm of male supremacy; it challenges the systematized sexual hatred by which men construct and defend their sex class—both socially and in private. Today's forbidden language of sex speaks of male-over-female sexual domination and wants it dead. Today's forbidden language of sex analyzes what sex is as men have defined it and as men as a class want it and as men as a class have it. Today's forbidden language of sex is discourse about the meaning of the formerly forbidden language of sex.

Today's forbidden language of sex is dangerous to male supremacy, so of course it must be stopped. That is the central reason the feminist critique of pornography is under attack—primarily by writers and editors and publishers. They say that feminist discourse on the meaning of pornography is antisex and prudish and moralizing, and it leaves no room for the passions and the warfare that are said to be the stuff of mutual heterosexual desire. They say that the feminist movement against pornography is mistaken because pornography is fantasy not action, and just as victimless as prostitution. They say that feminist organizing against the degrading and sexist values in pornography only serves the interests of the far Right and will bring down state censorship, probably on feminists first. They say the problem is the quality of the pornography, and feminists who don't like it should be busy producing good porn to drive out the bad. They say, simply, "I am a real woman, I want to be taken, I like sex hostile, so get off my case." And in the face of a ten-billion-dollar-a-year pornography industry with links to organized crime, forced prostitution, sexual slavery, and this writers' congress,* some of them, women

---

* Which had accepted a $3,000 grant from the Playboy Foundation.

writers and editors and publishers, say, "You feminists against pornography are more of a threat to me, more of an infringement on my freedom, than the pornographers." It is not necessary for the male-supremacist state, its laws and repressive machinery, to silence the new forbidden language of sex. Writers, editors, and publishers already do it—by distorting, and discrediting, and disavowing the radical-feminist case against male-supremacist sexuality.

Over the past ten or twelve years, radical feminists have developed a content analysis of pornography. At the core of that analysis is a new way of looking at pornography: as a window into acculturated male sexuality: what it is, what it desires, what it does, and why. The picture pornography exposes is not a pretty one; pornography reveals in the sexuality of the men for whom it is made an addiction to force and coercion for arousal, eroticized racial hatred, a despisal of the female, a fetishizing of erection and devotion to penetration, an obsession with interpersonal power differentials, an eroticized commitment to violence—and through it all an ugly striving to assert masculinity over and against women. About the only aspects of male sexuality that one can't discern by studying pornography are those that have not been acculturated to respond to pornography—whatever those variations might be. But apart from that, pornography is about the most reliable evidence that we have about male sexual identity and the sexuality that reinforces it and the values that construct it.

There used to be a clearer awareness about the relationship between pornography and male sexual arousal. Nowadays, that relationship is more hidden, less talked about, even though the pornography is more visible. It is almost as if the pornography industry and its defenders are truly embarrassed to admit that some of the stuff they turn out could conceivably excite some man somewhere to sexual arousal. So pornography is defended as "speech," as "art," as the workings of a free press, as the product of free enterprise, as the symbol of a free society, as "liberated" sex—meanwhile what is left unsaid is that the sexuality of men as a class is ravenous for the stuff, and that what sells sells because it creates and feeds men's sexual appetites. All pornography exists because it connects to some man's sexuality somewhere. There's no other reason.

Many men—knowing intimately the correspondence between the values in their sexuality and in pornography—share the anxiety that the feminist antipornography movement is really an attack on male sexuality. These nervous and angry men are quite correct: The feminist antipornography movement really does hold men accountable for the consequences to real women of their sexual proclivities. The feminist antipornography movement really is a refusal to believe that a man's divine right is to force sex, to use another person's body as if it were a hollow cantaloupe, a slap of liver, and to injure and debilitate for the sake of his gratification.

When one looks at any pornography, one sees what helps some man somewhere feel aroused, feel filled with maleness and devoid of all that is nonmale. When one looks at pornography, one sees what is necessary to sustain the social structure of male contempt for female flesh whereby men achieve a sense of themselves as male. When one looks at pornography, one sees what men as a class need to feel sexed; one sees what men as a class need to feel real.

Pornography tells lies about women. But pornography tells the truth about men.

Pornography and Freedom

There is a widespread belief that sexual freedom is an idea whose time has come. Many people believe that in the last few decades we have gotten more and more of it—that sexual freedom is something you can carve out against the forces of sexual repressiveness, and that significant gains have been won, gains we dare not give up lest we backslide into the sexual dark ages, when there wasn't sexual freedom, there was only repression.

Indeed many things seem to have changed. But if you look closely at what is supposed to be sexual freedom, you can become very confused. Let's say, for instance, you understand that a basic principle of sexual freedom is that people should be free to be sexual and that one way to guarantee that freedom is to make sure that sex be free from imposed restraint. That's not a bad idea, but if you happen to look at a magazine photograph in which a woman is bound and gagged and lashed down on a plank with her genital area open to the camera, you might well wonder: Where is the freedom from restraint? where's the sexual freedom?

Let's say you understand that people should be free to be sexual and that one way to guarantee that freedom is to make sure people can feel good about themselves and each other sexually. That's not a bad idea. But if you happen to read random passages from books such as the following, you could be quite perplexed:

"Baby, you're gonna get fucked tonight like you ain't never been fucked before," he hissed evilly down at her as she struggled fruitlessly against her bonds. The man wanted only to abuse and ravish her till she was totally broken and subservient to him. He knelt between her wide-spread legs and gloated over the cringing little pussy he was about to ram his cock into.[1]

And here's another:

He pulled his prick out of her cunt and then grabbed his belt from his pants. He seemed to be in a wild frenzy at that moment. He slapped the belt in the air and then the leather ripped through the girl's tender flesh. "Sir, just tell me what it is you want and I'll do it." "Fuck you, you little two-bit whore! I don't need nothin' from a whore!" The belt sliced across her flesh again and then she screamed, "I'm willing!" "That's just it! You're willing! You're a whore and you are an abomination . . ."[2]

Passages such as these might well make you wonder: Where are the good feelings about each other's body? where's the sexual freedom?

Let's say you understand that people should be free to be sexual and that one way to guarantee that freedom is to make sure people are free from sexualized hate and degradation. But let's say you come upon a passage such as this:

Reaching into his pocket for the knife again, Ike stepped just inches away from Burl's outstretched body. He slid the knife under Burl's cock and balls, letting the sharp edge of the blade lightly scrape the underside of Burl's nutsack. As if to reassert his power over Burl, Ike grabbed one of the bound man's tautly stretched pecs, clamping down hard over Burl's tit and muscle, latching on as tight as he could. He pushed on the knife, pressing the blade into Burl's skin as hard as possible without cutting him. "Now, you just let us inside that tight black asshole of yours, boy, or else we're gonna cut this off and feed it to the cattle!" [3]

After reading that, you might well ask: Where's the freedom from hatred? where's the freedom from degradation? where's the sexual freedom?

Let's say you understand people should be free to be sexual and that one way to guarantee that freedom is to make sure people are not punished for the individuality of their sexuality. And then you find a magazine showing page after page of bodies with their genitals garroted in baling wire and leather thongs, with their genitals tied up and tortured, with heavy weights suspended from rings that pierce their genitals, and the surrounding text makes clear that this mutilation and punishment are experienced as sex acts. And you might wonder in your mind: Why must this person suffer punishment in order to experience sexual feelings? why must this person be humiliated and disciplined and whipped and beaten until he bleeds in order to have access to his homoerotic passion? why have the Grand Inquisitor's most repressive and sadistic torture techniques become what people do to each other and call sex? where's the sexual freedom?

If you look back at the books and magazines and movies that have been produced in this country in the name of sexual freedom over the past decade, you've got to wonder: *Why has sexual freedom come to look so much like sexual repression? why has sexual freedom come to look so much like unfreedom?* The answer, I believe, has to do with the relationship between freedom and justice, and specifically the relationship between *sexual* freedom and *sexual* justice. When we think of freedom in any other sense, we think of freedom as *the result* of justice.

We know that there can't truly *be* any freedom until justice has happened, until justice exists. For any people in history who have struggled for freedom, those people have understood that their freedom exists on the future side of justice. The notion of freedom *prior to* justice is understood to be meaningless. Whenever people do not have freedom, they have understood freedom to be that which you arrive at by achieving justice. If you told them they should try to have their freedom without there being justice, they would laugh in your face. Freedom *always* exists on the far side of justice. That's perfectly understood—except when it comes to sex.

The popular concept of sexual freedom in this country has never meant sexual justice. Sexual-freedom advocates have cast the issue only in terms of having sex that is free from suppression and restraint. Practically speaking, that has meant advocacy of sex that is free from institutional interference; sex that is free from being constrained by legal, religious, and medical ideologies; sex that is free from any outside intervention. Sexual freedom on a more personal level has meant sex that is free from fear, guilt, and shame—which in practical terms has meant advocacy of sex that is free from value judgments, sex that is free from responsibility, sex that is free from consequences, sex that is free from ethical distinctions, sex that is essentially free from any obligation to take into account in one's consciousness that the other person is a *person*. In order to free sex from fear, guilt, and shame, it was thought that institutional restrictions on sex needed to be overthrown, but in fact what needed to be overthrown was any vestige of an interpersonal ethic in which people would be real to one another; for once people are real to one another, the consequences of one's acts matter deeply and personally; and particularly in the case of sex, one risks perceiving the consequences of one's acts in ways that feel *bad* because they do not feel *right*. This entire moral-feeling level of sexuality, therefore, needed to be undone. And it was undone, in the guise of an assault on institutional suppression.

Sexual freedom has never really meant that individuals should have sexual self-determination, that individuals should be free to experience the integrity of their own bodies and be free to act out of that integrity in a way that is totally within their own right to choose. Sexual freedom has never really meant that people should have absolute sovereignty over their own erotic being. And the reason for this is simple: Sexual freedom has never really been about *sexual justice between men and women*. It has been about maintaining men's superior status, men's power over women; and it has been about sexualizing women's inferior status, men's subordination of women. Essentially, sexual freedom has been about preserving a sexuality that preserves male supremacy.

What makes male supremacy so insidious, so pervasive, such a seemingly permanent component of all our precious lives, is the fact that erection can be conditioned to it. And orgasm can be habituated to it. There's a cartoon; it's from *Penthouse*: A man and woman are in bed. He's on top, fucking her. The caption reads: "I can't come unless you pretend to be unconscious." The joke could as well have taken any number of variations: "I can't get hard unless— I can't fuck unless— I can't get turned on unless— I can't feel anything sexual unless— . . ." Then fill in the blanks: "Unless I am possessing you. Unless I am superior to you. Unless I am in control of you. Unless I am humiliating you. Unless I am hurting you. Unless I have broken your will."

Once sexuality is stuck in male supremacy, all the forms of unjust power at the heart of it become almost physically addictive. All the stuff of our primitive fight-or-flight reflexes—a pounding heart, a hard sweat, heaving lungs—these are all things the body does when it is in terror, when it is lashing out in rage, and these are all things it is perfectly capable of doing during sex acts that are terrifying and sex acts that are vengeful. Domination and subordination—the very essence of injustice and unfreedom—have become culturally eroticized, and we are supposed to believe that giving eroticized domination and subordination free expression is the fullest flowering of sexual freedom.

Prepubescent boys get erections in all kinds of apparently nonsexual situations—being terrified, being in physical danger, being punished, moving perilously fast, simply being called on to recite in class. A boy's body's dilemma, as he grows older, as he learns more about the cultural power signified by the penis and how it is supposed to function in male-supremacist sex, is how to produce erections reliably in explicitly hetero-sexual contexts. His body gets a great deal of help. All around him is a culture in which rage and dread and hazard and aggression are made aphrodisiacs. And women's bodies are made the butt of whatever works to get it up.*

The sexuality of male supremacy is viscerally committed to domina-tion and subordination, because those are the terms on which it learned to feel, to feel anything sexual at all. Its heart pounds and its blood rushes and its autonomic nervous system surges at the thought and/or the action of forced sex, bullying sex, violent sex, injurious sex, humili-ating sex, hostile sex, murderous sex. The kind of sex that puts the other person in their place. The kind of sex that keeps the other person *other.* The kind of sex that makes you know you're in the presence of someone who is palpably a man.

Some of us know how male-supremacist sexuality feels better than do others. Some of us know how that sexuality feels inside because we do it, or we have done it, or we would like to do it, or we would like to do it more than we get a chance to. It's the sexuality that makes us feel powerful, virile, in control. Some of us have known how that sexuality feels when someone else is doing it to us, someone who is having sex with us, someone whose body is inhabited by it, someone who is experiencing its particular imperative and having male-supremacist sex against our flesh. And some of us don't really know this sexuality di-rectly; in fact our bodies haven't adapted to male supremacy very suc-cessfully at all—it is not the sexuality that moves us, that touches us, that

---

* See "Sexual Objectification and Male Supremacy," pp. 51–53.

---

comes anywhere near feeling as good as we imagine we want our sexual feelings to feel. We don't recognize a longing for anything like it in our own bodies, and we've been lucky so far—very lucky—not to have experienced it *against* our bodies. Nonetheless, we know that it exists; and the more we know about pornography, the more we know what it looks like.

Pornography and Male Supremacy

Male-supremacist sexuality is important to pornography, and pornography is important to male supremacy. Pornography *institutionalizes* the sexuality that both embodies and enacts male supremacy. Pornography says about that sexuality, "Here's how": Here's how to act out male supremacy in sex. Here's how the action should go. Here are the acts that impose power over and against another body. And pornography says about that sexuality, "Here's who": Here's who you should do it to and here's who she is: your whore, your piece of ass, yours. Your penis is a weapon, her body is your target. And pornography says about that sexuality, "Here's why": Because men are masters, women are slaves; men are superior, women are subordinate; men are real, women are objects; men are sex machines, women are sluts.

Pornography institutionalizes male supremacy the way segregation institutionalizes white supremacy. It is a practice embodying an ideology of biological superiority; it is an institution that both expresses that ideology and enacts that ideology—makes it the reality that people believe is true, keeps it that way, keeps people from knowing any other possibility, keeps certain people powerful by keeping certain people *down.*

Pornography also *eroticizes* male supremacy. It makes dominance and subordination feel like sex; it makes hierarchy feel like sex; it makes force and violence feel like sex; it makes hate and terrorism feel like sex; it makes inequality feel like sex. Pornography keeps sexism sexy. It keeps

Pornography and Male Supremacy

sexism *necessary* for some people to have sexual feelings. It makes reciprocity make you go limp. It makes mutuality leave you cold. It makes tenderness and intimacy and caring make you feel like you're going to disappear into a void. It makes justice the opposite of erotic; it makes injustice a sexual thrill.

Pornography exploits every experience in people's lives that *imprisons* sexual feelings—pain, terrorism, punishment, dread, shame, powerlessness, self-hate—and would have you believe that it *frees* sexual feelings. In fact the sexual freedom represented by pornography is the freedom of men to act sexually in ways that keep sex a basis for inequality.

You can't have authentic sexual freedom without sexual justice. It is only freedom for those in power; the powerless cannot be free. Their experience of sexual freedom becomes but a delusion borne of complying with the demands of the powerful. Increased sexual freedom under male supremacy has had to mean an increased tolerance for sexual practices that are predicated on eroticized injustice between men and women: treating women's bodies or body parts as merely sexual objects or things; treating women as utterly submissive masochists who enjoy pain and humiliation and who, if they are raped, enjoy it; treating women's bodies to sexualized beating, mutilation, bondage, dismemberment.... Once you have sexualized inequality, once it is a learned and internalized prerequisite for sexual arousal and sexual gratification, then anything goes. And that's what sexual freedom means on this side of sexual justice.

Pornography and Homophobia

Homophobia is absolutely integral to the system of sexualized male supremacy. Cultural homophobia expresses a whole range of antifemale revulsion: It expresses contempt for men who are sexual with men because they are believed to be "treated like a woman" in sex. It expresses contempt for women who are sexual with women just *because* they are women and also because they are perceived to be a rebuke to the primacy of the penis.

But cultural homophobia is not merely an expression of woman hating; it also works to protect men from the sexual aggression of other men. Homophobia keeps men doing to women what they would not want done to themselves. There's not the same sexual harassment of men that there is of women on the street or in the workplace or in the university; there's not nearly the same extent of rape; there's not the same demeaned social caste that is sexualized, as it is for women. And that's thanks to homophobia: Cultural homophobia keeps men's sexual aggression directed toward women. Homophobia keeps men acting in concert as male supremacists so that they won't be perceived as an appropriate target for male-supremacist sexual treatment. Male supremacy *requires* homophobia in order to keep men safe from the sexual aggression of men. Imagine this country *without* homophobia: A woman raped every three minutes *and a man* raped every three minutes. Homophobia that keeps that statistic at a "manageable" level. The system is not foolproof, of course. There are boys who have been sexually molested by men. There are men who have been brutalized in sexual relationships with their male lovers, and they too have a memory of men's sexual violence. And there are many men in prison who are subject to the same sexual terrorism that women live with almost all the time. But for the most part—happily—homophobia serves male supremacy by protecting "real men" from sexual assault by other real men.

Pornography is one of the major enforcers of cultural homophobia. Pornography is rife with gay-baiting and effemiphobia. Portrayals of allegedly lesbian "scenes" are a staple of heterosexual pornography: The women with each other are there for the male viewer, the male voyeur; there is not the scantest evidence that they are there for each other. Through so-called men's-sophisticate magazines—the "skin" magazines—

pornographers outdo one another in their attacks against feminists, who are typically derided as lesbians—"sapphic" at best, "bulldykes" at worst. The innuendo that a man is a "fairy" or a "faggot" is, in pornography, a kind of dare or a challenge to prove his cocksmanship. And throughout pornography, the male who is perceived to be the passive orifice in sex is tainted with the disdain that "normally" belongs to women.

Meanwhile gay male pornography, which often appears to present an idealized, all-male, superbutch world, also contains frequent derogatory references to women, or to feminized males. In order to give vent to male sexual aggression and sadism in homosexual pornography and also to circumvent the cultural stigma that ordinarily attaches to men who are "treated like a woman" in sex, gay male pornography has developed several specific "codes." One such code is that a man who is "capable" of withstanding "discipline"—extremely punishing bondage, humiliation, and fistfucking, for instance—is deemed to have achieved a kind of supermasculinity, almost as if the sexual violence his body ingests from another man enhances his own sexual identity as a man. (This is quite the reverse in heterosexual pornography, where sexual sadism against a woman simply confirms her in her subordinate status.) Another code common in gay male pornography, one found frequently in films, is that if a man is shown being assfucked, he will generally be shown assfucking someone else in turn—this to avoid the connotation that he is at all feminized by being fucked. Still another code in gay male pornography is that depictions of mutuality are not sustained for very long without an intimation or explicit scene of force or coercion—so you don't go limp out of boredom or anxiety that you've been suckered into a scene where there's no raw male power present.

There is, not surprisingly, an intimate connection between the male supremacy in both heterosexual and homosexual pornography and the woman hating and femiphobia in them both as well. That connection is male-supremacist sex—the social power of men over women acted out as eroticized domination and subordination. The difference is that gay male pornography invents a way for men to be the *objects* of male-supremacist sex without seeming to be its *victims*. In its own special fashion, gay male pornography keeps men safe from male-supremacist sex—by holding out the promise that you'll come away from it more a man.

Needless to say, for heterosexual men who don't buy this, it's repellent and a crock. Needless to say, for homosexual men who *do* buy into this, it can become a really important part of one's sexual identity as a gay man. Because if you think the problem facing you is that your masculinity is in doubt because you're queer, then the promise of gay male pornography looks like forgiveness and redemption. Not to mention what it feels like: communion with true virility.

Pornography and Men

Now this is the situation of men within male supremacy: Whether we are straight or gay, we have been looking for a sexual freedom that is utterly specious, and we have been looking for it through pornography, which perpetuates the very domination and subordination that stand in the way of sexual justice. Whether we are straight or gay, we have been looking for a notion of freedom that leaves out women; we have been looking for a sexuality that preserves men's power over women. So long as that is what we strive for, we cannot possibly feel freely, and no one can be free. Whatever sexual freedom might be, it must be after justice.

I want to speak directly to those of us who live in male supremacy as men, and I want to speak specifically to those of us who have come to understand that pornography does make sexism sexy; that pornography does make male supremacy sexy; and that pornography does define what is sexy in terms of domination and subordination, in terms that serve *us as men*—whether we buy it or not, whether we buy into it or not—because it serves male supremacy, which is exactly what it is for.

I want to speak to those of us who live in this setup as men and who recognize—in the world and in our very own selves—the power pornography can have over our lives: It can make men believe that anything sexy is good. It can make men believe that our penises are like weapons. It can make men believe—for some moments of orgasm—that we are just like the men in pornography: virile, strong, tough, maybe cruel. It can make men believe that if you take it away from us, we won't have sexual feelings.

But I want to speak also to those of us who live in this setup as men and who recognize the power that pornography has over the lives of women: because it can make us believe that women by nature are whores; because it can make us believe that women's body parts belong to us— separately, part by part—instead of to a whole real other person; because it can make us believe that women want to be raped, enjoy being damaged by us, deserve to be punished; because it can make us believe that women are an alien species, completely different from us so that we can be completely different from them, not as human as us so that we can be human, not as real as us so that we can be men. I want to talk to those of us who know in our guts that pornography can make us believe all of that. We know because we've watched it happen to men around us. We know because it has happened in us.

And what I want to say is simply this: We've got to be about making some serious changes, and we've got to get busy and *act*. If we sit around and don't do anything, then we become the ones who are keeping things the way they are. If we sit around and all we do is intellectual and emotional dithering, then we stay in the ranks of those who are the passive enforcers of male supremacy. If we don't take seriously the fact that pornography is a radical political issue and an issue about *us* and if we don't make serious progress in the direction of *what we're going to do about it*, then we've just gone over to the wrong side of the fight— the morally wrong, historically wrong side of a struggle that is a ground swell, a grass-roots *people's* movement against sexual injustice.

We've got to be telling our sons that if a man gets off by putting women down, *it's not okay.*

We've got to be telling merchants that if they peddle women's bodies and lives for men's consumption and entertainment, *it's not okay.*

We've got to be telling other men that if you let the pornographers lead you by the nose (or any other body part) into believing that women exist to be tied up and hung up and beaten and raped, *it's not okay.*

We've got to be telling the pornographers—Larry Flynt and Bob Guccione and Hugh Hefner and Al Goldstein and all the rest—that whatever they think they're doing in our names as men, as entertainment for men, for the sake of some delusion of so-called manhood . . . well, it's not okay. It's not okay with *us.*

Freedom and Equality

Historically, when people have not had justice and when people have not had freedom, they have had only the material reality of injustice and unfreedom. When freedom and justice don't exist, they're but a dream and a vision, an abstract idea longed for. You can't really know what justice would be like or what freedom would feel like. You can only know how it feels *not* to have them, and what it feels like to hope, to imagine, to desire them with a passion. Sexual freedom is an idea whose time has *not* come. It can't possibly be truly experienced until there is sexual justice. And sexual justice is incompatible with a definition of freedom that is based on the subordination of women.

Equality is still a radical idea. It makes some people very angry. It also gives some people hope.

When equality is an idea whose time has come, we will perhaps know sex with justice, we will perhaps know passion with compassion, we will perhaps know ardor and affection with honor. In that time, when the integrity within everyone's body and the whole personhood of each person is celebrated whenever two people touch, we will perhaps truly know the freedom to be sexual in a world of real equality.

According to pornography, you can't get there from here. According to male supremacy, you should not even want to try.

Some of us want to go there. Some of us want to be there. And we know that the struggle will be difficult and long. But we know that the passion for justice cannot be denied. And someday—*someday*—there will be both justice and freedom for each person—and thereby for us all.

Confronting Pornography as a
Civil-Rights Issue

How can we end the injustice that is based on sex? How can there be sexual justice?

There are many necessary ways to achieve sexual justice in society. The law ought to be an important one. Justice, after all, is supposed to be among the law's primary functions. But the law has had a very sorry record on that score. Historically, laws have served to perpetuate injustice—slavery, for example—as often as, or more often than, they have served to undo it. And laws about sex have been especially unhelpful, for they tend to serve the interests of the powerful and betray those who are powerless. Rape laws, for instance, have maintained the right of husbands to rape. Obscenity laws have perpetuated a belief in the vileness of women's bodies and protected men from their sexual shame in relation to other men. Sodomy laws have legitimized the persecution of those whose very existence is felt to jeopardize men's hold on the superior status of their sex. If anything, law has functioned to defend male supremacy, to reinforce sexual injustice.

In the fall of 1983, in the city of Minneapolis, a new legal theory was invented that might actually defy male supremacy and materially effect some sexual justice. This legal theory was contained in antipornography legislation developed by radical feminists that would permit civil lawsuits against pornographers on the grounds that pornography is a violation of women's civil rights—because pornography subordinates women as a class and thereby creates sex discrimination.* I'm going to explain—step by step—how this civil-rights approach to pornography would work: how and why this legislation was developed, what it would and wouldn't do, and how it differs—both legally and politically—from obscenity law.

A Brief Background

The idea of confronting pornography as a civil-rights issue did not fall from the sky. It grew out of the outrage and frustration of over a decade of grass-roots feminist activism against pornography. The definitive history of this influential movement has yet to be written—but here's a sketch:

Activism in the women's movement on the issue of pornography can be traced back to September 1968, when women, led by a group called New York Radical Women, first "zapped" the Miss America Pageant in Atlantic City, with a day of songs, chants, and guerrilla theater protesting the contest's sexist and racist celebration of women as objects.[1] A rash of demonstrations against Hugh M. Hefner's Playboy empire soon followed— at Playboy Clubs across the country. One group of protesters, the Mountain

---

* See "Selected Bibliography: The Civil-Rights Antipornography Ordinance," pp. 221–225.

Moving Day Brigade, challenged Hefner's hegemony in these words:

We sisters join together to fight you, your Playboy empire and everything you represent, and we shall build instead a society in which women and men are free to relate to each other as equal human beings of dignity and worth. Until you no longer oppose this, you shall have no peace.[2]

Hefner, for his part, issued an in-house memo that got leaked to the nation:

These chicks are our natural enemy . . . It is time we do battle with them . . . What I want is a devastating piece that takes the militant feminists apart. They are unalterably opposed to the romantic boy-girl society that Playboy promotes . . . Let's go to it and make it a real winner.[3]

It was all-out war: the pornographers against women, women against the pornographers. In the next several years, there were to be scores of scattered feminist antipornography actions, including, for the first time, civil disobedience: In the spring of 1970, militant feminists seized and barricaded the executive offices of the avant-garde, Left/liberal Grove Press in New York City, partly as a protest against its publications that degraded women.[4]

The year 1976 marks a sort of flash point in the feminist antipornography movement. In February, a first-run theater in New York City's Times Square opened a movie called *Snuff*, which purported to show the actual murder of a woman for sexual entertainment. Hundreds of women and some men picketed the theater night after night. In the movie, a man kills then disembowels a woman and holds up her uterus as he appears to have an orgasm. Eventually, the gore was revealed to be simulated; but hoax or not, the movie sent out a message about women that was all too real. When *Snuff* rolled out into national distribution, it galvanized feminists to form local groups against pornography across the United States—the

---

largest of which, Women Against Violence in Pornography and Media (WAVPM), was based in San Francisco.

In June 1976, Atlantic Records erected a billboard in Los Angeles on Sunset Strip showing a woman bound and bruised saying "I'm 'Black and Blue' from The Rolling Stones—and I love it!" A group called Women Against Violence Against Women (WAVAW) protested and got the billboard taken down, then joined with California NOW in calling a national boycott against Atlantic, Warner Bros., and Elektra/Asylum records, demanding an end to these companies' violent and woman-hating album covers.[5]

When the June 1978 issue of Larry Flynt's *Hustler* magazine hit newsstands, it triggered another outburst of feminist protests coast-to-coast: Billing itself an "all-meat issue," the cover showed a naked woman being shoved head-first into a meat grinder—and extruded at the other end as raw hamburger.

The first feminist conference on pornography convened in San Francisco in November 1978, sponsored by WAVPM, and it launched the first Take Back the Night March—down San Francisco's pornography row in North Beach. A few months later, in October 1979, over 5,000 women and men marched against pornography in Times Square, organized by Women Against Pornography, originally a WAVPM spinoff. In the years thereafter, Take Back the Night marches and rallies have become an annual event in hundreds of cities and communities. Dozens of WAVAW chapters and many other groups sprang up in local protests against record-album jackets, pornography retailers, and other forms of media exploitation and violence against women. In addition, on hundreds of campuses, there were spontaneous demonstrations against fraternity and film-society showings of pornographic films, the sale of pornographic magazines in campus bookstores, and photographers soliciting for women to pose for *Playboy*.

This burgeoning grass-roots activism was accompanied by a surge of feminist writings that analyzed pornography as sexist, degrading, demeaning images and as woman-hating propaganda.[6] As feminists spoke out, more and more women came forward and told how men's use of pornography had been directly involved in their personal histories of incest, child sexual abuse, marital rape, battery, and other forms of sexual victimization, or how pornography had been used to "season" them into a life of prostitution. By the beginning of the 1980s, a new political analysis was emerging: a real-life–based comprehension of pornography as being somehow central to women's inferior social status—together with a sense of being utterly powerless against the resources of the huge pornography industry and its callous civil-libertarian defenders.

In addition to this background of feminist antipornography activism, the thinking behind the civil-rights antipornography law was influenced by:

• The increased distribution of pornography, due in part to technologic advances such as cable TV and the home video market.

• The wider availability of more and more violent and sadistic pornography. Acts were being photographed and sold that were heretofore unimaginable: torture, mutilation, sex with animals, vaginal penetration by knives, and so forth. Pornography production seemed to be racing to keep ahead of the satiation effect in consumers—trying to deliver a sex kick to sated would-be satyrs through more and more brutality against women.

• Social-science research designed to test hypotheses suggested by feminists' analysis of pornography. Controlled experiments were conducted with groups of "normal" college-age men, screened to eliminate "rape-prone" and "high-hostile" types. The experiments showed that in these average good joes, exposure to certain types of pornography produced significant effects such as increased levels of aggression and hostility, increased callousness toward women, and increased self-reported likelihood to rape if they thought they would not get caught.[7]

Pornography and Male Supremacy

• The escape of "Linda Lovelace," whose real name is Linda Marchiano. In her autobiography, the woman who starred in *Deep Throat*, the world's highest-grossing pornographic film, told how she had in fact been intimidated, beaten, and brutally bullied into performing for pornography by her pimp/husband—sometimes at gunpoint.[8] For several years Marchiano tried to get someone to help her take her case to court, but no one in the succession of male lawyers she appealed to thought anything could be done. Then, beginning in June 1980, when Linda Marchiano joined with Women Against Pornography in calling for a nationwide boycott of *Deep Throat*, Andrea Dworkin, the radical feminist writer, and Catharine A. MacKinnon, at the time a feminist lawyer teaching at Yale Law School, attempted to help Marchiano take legal action against the gross injustice she had experienced. The statutes of limitation in the crimes of abuse that had happened to her had by now expired—as indeed they usually do before a woman so sexually victimized can recover enough emotionally to be able to cope with a prosecution. Meanwhile the film of her coerced performance continued to earn its owners and distributors millions and millions of dollars.[9]

• The backlash reaction against feminist antipornography activists from pornographers and defenders of pornography. Feminists who had organized and written against pornography during the seventies had had no idea just *how* central pornography was to the system of men's social power over and against women. But the misogyny and vehemence with which their movement began to be denounced and reviled, in pornography magazines and elsewhere, became a tangible tip-off that in confronting the sexual domination of women in pornography they had unwittingly hit the jugular vein—or perhaps, more accurately, the nerve center—of male supremacy.

Quite coincidentally, in Minneapolis, Minnesota, there was another history of activism against pornography going on. This was not a feminist-inspired movement; it was, rather, a coalition of neighborhood groups

142

that were organizing to confront the way the pornography industry was operating in their city. These citizens were angry about the fact that "adult" book and video stores were being located mostly in poor areas and in communities where blacks, Native Americans, and other people of color lived, saturating these neighborhoods with pornography, with a resulting increase in crime and deterioration of the neighborhood. For them pornography was a community issue, a class issue, and a racial issue: They wanted to stop pornography's erosion of the quality of their lives, the land values where they lived, and their physical security. Local citizens groups had tried for over seven years to tackle the problem of pornography in neighborhoods through zoning laws. But these zoning laws had been struck down as unconstitutional, because, as a woman judge on the Minnesota state supreme court opined, they inconvenienced anyone who wanted to buy the stuff; he'd have to travel too far, which would be a nasty incursion on his First Amendment rights. So by the fall of 1983, the Minneapolis City Council was in the process of deliberating on a new zoning law—one that would circumvent this judge's ruling by establishing eight "adult bookstore" zones handily dispersed throughout the city. The issue for neighborhood organizers, however, remained the same: Into *whose* neighborhood would the pornography be zoned?

At the time of these deliberations, Andrea Dworkin and Catharine A. MacKinnon just happened to be in Minneapolis coteaching a course on pornography and law at the University of Minnesota Law School. The two were a formidable team:

• Catharine A. MacKinnon—a feminist lawyer, teacher, writer, and activist—is the constitutional-law scholar who pioneered the legal theory that defined and established sexual harassment as a legal term of art and an actionable form of sex discrimination.[10] Before coming to Minnesota as associate professor teaching sex discrimination and constitutional law, she had taught at Yale, Harvard, and Stanford law schools.

• Andrea Dworkin—at the time a visiting professor in women's studies and law at the University of Minnesota—is a feminist writer, activist, and impassioned public speaker who had addressed scores of Take Back the Night rallies beginning with the first, in San Francisco. She had published extensively about pornography as a women's issue since 1974 [11] and had spoken at colleges and demonstrations in the late seventies on "Pornography: The New Terrorism." [12] Pornography plays a role in both causing and justifying all forms of sexual abuse, she believed, and therefore it plays a role in creating and maintaining the civil inferiority of women.[13] "Simply put," according to Dworkin, "if raping women is entertainment, what are women's lives worth?"

In October 1983, the Neighborhood Pornography Task Force convinced Dworkin and MacKinnon to appear before the Minneapolis City Council Zoning and Planning Committee to testify about the new zoning ordinance. They testified that they were *opposed* to the zoning approach—because it did absolutely nothing to remedy the real injury that pornography does. Speaking first, Dworkin broached a feminist legal analysis that "[p]ornography is an abuse of the civil rights of women. It is an absolute repudiation of our right to equality under the law and as citizens of this country." [14] Then MacKinnon told the committee, "I suggest that you consider that pornography, as it subordinates women to men, is a form of discrimination on the basis of sex" [15] and proposed that instead of zoning pornography—which indicates, said Dworkin, "that property matters and property values matter but that women don't" [16]—the city could deal with pornography through an amendment to its laws prohibiting sex discrimination. Quite improbably and unexpectedly, the zoning committee unanimously moved to direct the city attorney to pursue this civil-rights approach. Within weeks, the City of Minneapolis hired Dworkin and MacKinnon as consultants—to draft a law recognizing that pornography violates women's civil rights and to organize public hearings that would become a legislative record showing how women's rights are violated by the production and consumption of pornography.

The law they drafted was an amendment to the Minneapolis Civil

Rights Ordinance. Essentially it would give the victims of pornography *a chance to fight back*. For the first time in history, this law would allow a woman to try to prove that she had been injured by having pornography forced on her, by being coerced into a pornographic performance, or because pornography was used in some sexual assault on her. It would also allow a woman to sue traffickers in pornography on the basis of the harm pornography does to the civil rights of women as a class. This law, which became widely known as the Dworkin/MacKinnon Civil-Rights Antipornography Ordinance, was "based on the idea—like the principle underlying the Fourteenth Amendment—that women have *rights* and that those rights are abrogated by systematic sexual subordination."[17]

In December of 1983, there were two days of public hearings on the proposed Ordinance in Minneapolis. Researchers testified; victims testified; people who worked with victims of rape, battery, and child sexual assault testified. It was the first time in history that any legislative body had ever listened to real people's experience of their victimization through pornography.[18] The hearings transcript includes the testimony of Linda Marchiano, who as "Linda Lovelace" was beaten and forced into performing in the film *Deep Throat*. Here is part of her testimony. At the time of the filming, she was married to a man named Chuck Traynor, whom she calls Mr. Traynor.

During the filming of *Deep Throat*, actually after the first day, I suffered a brutal beating in my room for smiling on the set. It was a hotel room and the whole crew was in one room, there was at least twenty people partying, music going, laughing, and having a good time. Mr. Traynor started to bounce me off the walls. I figured out of twenty people, there might be one human being that would do something to help me and I was screaming for help, I was being beaten, I was being kicked around and again bounced off the walls. And all of a sudden the room next door became very quiet. Nobody, not one person came to help me.

The greatest complaint the next day is the fact that there was bruises on my body. So many people say that in *Deep Throat* I have a smile on my face and I look as though I am really enjoying myself. No one ever asked me how those bruises got on my body.[19]

At another point in her testimony, Linda Marchiano said:

Mr. Traynor suggested the thought that I do films with a D-O-G and I told him that I wouldn't do it. I suffered a brutal beating, he claims he suffered embarrassment because I wouldn't do it.

We then went to another porno studio, one of the sleaziest ones I have ever seen, and then this guy walked in with his animal and I again started crying. I started crying. I said I am not going to do this and they were all very persistent, the two men involved in making the pornographic film and Mr. Traynor himself. And I started to leave and go outside of the room where they make these films and when I turned around there was all of a sudden a gun displayed on the desk and having seen the coarseness and the callousness of the people involved in pornography, I knew that I would have been shot and killed.

Needless to say the film was shot and still is one of the hardest ones for me to deal with today.[20]

The Four Causes of Action

The Civil-Rights Antipornography Ordinance is a civil law, unlike obscenity laws, which are criminal. Under a criminal law, someone can be tried and sentenced to go to jail if they commit a crime. But under a civil law, someone can be sued and ordered to pay money (which is called damages) or to stop doing something that they're doing (which is called an injunction).

The antipornography ordinance would allow a person access to the local human-rights commission and the civil court if they have a complaint under any of four causes of action. One of these causes of action is called **coercion into pornography**. This cause of action is one that Linda Marchiano could use even though the film *Deep Throat* was made many years ago, because the Ordinance would apply to the last "appearance or sale" of the film made of her coerced performance and *Deep Throat* is still for sale just about everywhere. Linda Marchiano testified in Minneapolis that "every time someone watches that film, they are watching me being raped." [21] The movie is in effect a filmed document of her coerced performances of sex acts.

Today, any movie may be made of any rape and then sold on the market as sexual entertainment. The rape, if the victim is very lucky, could be prosecuted, but the movie is considered "protected speech" under current law. In the last several years, rape-crisis centers have increasingly encountered rapes that have been photographed, and the photographs are being sold. Under current law, nothing can be done to remove the photographs from sale. But the Civil-Rights Antipornography Ordinance is written so that a person whose rape is photographed or who is coerced into performing for pornography has the right to file a complaint with a human-rights commission or bring a civil suit into court. If they successfully prove their case, they could collect money damages from the whole chain of profit, and that person could also get the pornography made from their coercion off the market in the locality where the Ordinance is in force.

If you know what happens to women victims in rape trials, you have some idea how difficult it is for any woman to prove that she did not consent to an act of forced sex. So imagine the difficulty of proving that you were coerced into performing for pornography when what you were forced to do was to act as if you were thoroughly enjoying what was happening to you. Recognizing that many women trying to use the coercion cause of action would be up against serious pretrial challenges, Dworkin and MacKinnon wrote into the Ordinance a list of "facts or conditions" that cannot in and of themselves be used by the pornographers to get a coercion case dismissed. This list includes "that the person is or has ever been a prostitute," because, among other reasons, it is virtually impossible for a prostitute to get a rape conviction. The list also includes "that the person is connected by blood or marriage to anyone involved in or related to the making of the pornography"; "Linda Lovelace," for example, was married—by force—to the man who was her pimp and torturer. The list also includes "that the person signed a contract . . ."; as Andrea Dworkin has said, "If you can force someone to fuck a dog, you can force them to sign a contract." The complete list includes thirteen items, a virtual catalog of smears used against women's veracity in court:

Proof of one or more of the following facts or conditions shall not, without more, preclude a finding of coercion:

a. that the person is a woman; or

b. that the person is or has been a prostitute; or

c. that the person has attained the age of majority; or

d. that the person is connected by blood or marriage to anyone involved in or related to the making of the pornography; or

e. that the person has previously had, or been thought to have had, sexual relations with anyone, including anyone involved in or related to the making of the pornography; or

f. that the person has previously posed for sexually explicit pictures with or for anyone, including anyone involved in or related to the making of the pornography; or

g. that anyone else, including a spouse or other relative, has given permission on the person's behalf; or

h. that the person actually consented to a use of a performance that is then changed into pornography; or

i. that the person knew that the purpose of the acts or events in question was to make pornography; or

j. that the person showed no resistance or appeared to cooperate actively in the photographic sessions or events that produced the pornography; or

k. that the person signed a contract, or made statements affirming a willingness to cooperate in the production of the pornography; or

l. that no physical force, threats, or weapons were used in the making of the pornography; or

m. that the person was paid or otherwise compensated.[22]

This list was mistakenly interpreted by some opponents of the bill as implying that women cannot ever consent. That's not what this list means at all. In a civil trial for coercion, the burden of proof is on the plaintiff, who must prove that she was actually coerced; and the defendants (the pornographers) can use every means at their disposal to prove that the plaintiff participated willingly. But the legal meaning of this list is that just because a woman is a prostitute or married to the producer or signed a release and so forth, that's not grounds for throwing a case of alleged coercion out of court before it can be tried.

Many people don't realize how pornography actually functions in the lives of its victims. They think of pornography as simply some pictures that some lonely guy masturbates to now and then. But that's not entirely accurate. In fact there are many women on whom pornography is forced, sometimes by husbands, boyfriends, or lovers, and many women who are assaulted in such a way that pornography is directly involved in the assault. For instance, in a random survey of women in San Francisco,[23] 10 percent of the women interviewed said they had been upset by a husband or lover who was pressuring them into doing something that they had seen in pornographic pictures, movies, or books. These are some of the things they said their husbands or boyfriends had asked them to do:

It was physical slapping and hitting. It wasn't a turn-on; it was more a feeling of being used as an object. What was most upsetting was that he thought it would be a turn-on.

My husband enjoys pornographic movies. He tries to get me to do things he finds exciting in movies. They include twosomes and threesomes. I always refuse. Also, I was always upset with his ideas about putting objects in my vagina, until I learned this is not as deviant as I used to think. He used to force me or put whatever he wanted into me.

He forced me to go down on him. He said he'd been going to porno movies. He'd seen this and wanted me to do it. He also wanted to pour champagne on my vagina. I got beat up because I didn't want to do it. He pulled my hair and slapped me around. After that I went ahead and did it, but there was no feeling in it.

This guy had seen a movie where a woman was being made love to by dogs. He suggested that some of his friends had a dog and we should have a party and set the dog loose on the women. He wanted me to put a muzzle on the dog and put some sort of stuff on my vagina so that the dog would lick there.

My old man and I went to a show that had lots of tying up and anal intercourse. We came home and proceeded to make love. He went out and got two belts. He tied my feet together with one, and with the other he kind of beat me. I was in the spirit, I really went along with it. But when he tried to penetrate me anally, I couldn't take it, it was too painful. I managed to convey to him verbally to quit it. He did stop, but not soon enough to suit me. Then one time, he branded me. I still have a scar on my butt. He put a little wax initial thing on a hot plate and then stuck it on my ass when I was unaware.

My boyfriend and I saw a movie in which there was masochism. After that he wanted to gag me and tie me up. He was stoned, I was not. I was really shocked at his behavior. I was nervous and uptight. He literally tried to force me, after gagging me first. He snuck up behind me with a scarf. He was hurting me with it and I started getting upset. Then I realized it wasn't a joke. He grabbed me and shook me by my shoulders and brought out some ropes, and told me to relax, and that I would enjoy it. Then he started putting me down about my feelings about sex, and my inhibitedness. I started crying and struggling with him, got loose, and kicked him in the testicles, which forced him down on the couch. I ran out of the house. Next day he called and apologized, but that was the end of him.[24]

As mounting testimony from pornography victims makes clear, the distinction often made between "fantasy" and real behavior simply doesn't stand up in the world of pornography. If someone forces their fantasy on you, the fantasy is no longer an abstract mental event; and if someone acts out their fantasy of assaulting you, something really happens. Often such "fantasies," modeled after pictorial pornography, are modeled after what really happened to the real woman in the pornography.

In the Civil-Rights Antipornography Ordinance there is a second cause of action called **forcing pornography on a person**. As this cause of action is defined, any person who is forced to watch pornography at home, in a place of work or education, or in public is having their civil rights violated. The person can sue the perpetrator and any institution that lets the abuse occur (just as in cases of sexual harassment). The importance of this cause of action is obvious if you think about battery: There is more and more testimony coming from battered women and from women working in battered-women's shelters about the amount of sexual abuse that is generated in marriages by men who are using pornography. There is also increasing testimony about a growing incidence of pornography-linked sadism in the home, including rape by animals, branding, and maiming.

A third cause of action is called **assault or physical attack due to pornography**. This provision enables anyone who has been raped or injured directly as a result of the use of a specific piece of pornography to sue the perpetrator of the assault for damages. The victim of the assault can also sue anyone who made or sold the specific pornography for money damages and for an injunction against further sale of it in the locality where the law is in force.

A fourth cause of action is called **trafficking in pornography**. A kind of "class action" cause of action, it is based on the notion that pornography is a practice of sex discrimination in and of itself. The trafficking provision basically says that if material meets the definition of pornography in the law, it is sex discrimination by definition; and any woman, acting in behalf of all women, can sue to have it removed from the marketplace because of its impact on the civil status of all women. (But no material may be removed from sale under the trafficking provision without a trial *de novo*—a full court trial.) There is now a body of proof in the form of clinical evidence, social studies, research studies, and victim testimony that pornography produces hostility, bigotry, and aggression against women, and also attitudes and behaviors of sex discrimination. The words of the preface to the Ordinance summarize these findings:

Pornography is a systematic practice of exploitation and subordination based on sex that differentially harms and disadvantages women. The harm of pornography includes dehumanization, psychic assault, sexual exploitation, forced sex, forced prostitution, physical injury, and social and sexual terrorism and inferiority presented as entertainment. The bigotry and contempt pornography promotes, with the acts of aggression it fosters, diminish opportunities for equality of rights in employment, education, property, public accommodations, and public services; create public and private harassment, persecution, and denigration; promote injury and degradation such as rape, battery, sexual abuse of children, and prostitution, and inhibit just enforcement of laws against these acts; expose individuals who appear in pornography against their will to contempt, ridicule, hatred, humiliation, and embarrassment and target such women in particular for abuse and physical aggression; demean the reputations and diminish the occupational opportunities of individuals and groups on the basis of sex; contribute significantly to restricting women in particular from full exercise of citizenship and participation in the life of the community; lower the human dignity, worth, and civil status of women and damage mutual respect between the sexes; and undermine women's equal exercise of rights to speech and action guaranteed to all citizens under the [Constitutions] and [laws] of [place].[25]

Under the trafficking provision of the Ordinance, any woman has a cause of action acting against the subordination of women as a class through the sale and distribution of particular pornography. In addition, any man, child, or transsexual can also sue under this cause of action.

They must prove that the pornography has the same impact on their civil status that it has on the civil status of women. This would be easy for children, whose powerlessness in society is closely related to that of women. It would also be theoretically possible for black men and homosexual men, because there exists pornography about them that sexualizes the same kind of hatred and violence that are involved in lynching and gay-bashing.

The following words are from a man named Chuck, who, when he was twenty, after two painful years of marriage, separated from his wife and daughter and felt enormous rage toward women for a year. His words expose the great difference between the world that women live in and the world that men live in—and how pornography and sexual violence keep the civil status of those worlds different and unequal:

Then one night about a year after I split from my wife, I was out partyin' and drinkin' and smokin' pot. I'd shot up some heroin and done some downers and I went to a porno bookstore, put a quarter in the slot, and saw this porn movie. It was just a guy coming up from behind a girl and attacking her and raping her. That's when I started having rape fantasies.

When I seen that movie, it was like somebody lit a fuse from my childhood on up. When that fuse got to the porn movie, I exploded. I just went for it, went out and raped. It was like a little voice saying, "It's all right, it's all right, go ahead and rape and get your revenge; you'll never get caught. Go out and rip off some girls. It's all right; they even make movies of it." The movie was just like a big picture stand with words on it saying go out and do it, everybody's doin' it, even the movies.

So I just went out that night and started lookin'. I went up to this woman and grabbed her breast; then I got scared and ran. I went home and had the shakes real bad, and then I started likin' the feeling of getting even with all women.

The second one was at a college. I tried to talk to this girl and she gave me some off-the-wall story. I chased her into a bathroom and grabbed her and told her that if she screamed, I'd kill her. I had sex with her that lasted about five minutes. When I first attacked her I wasn't even turned on; I wanted to dominate her. When I saw her get scared and hurt, then I got turned on. I wanted her to feel like she'd been drug through mud.

Pornography and Male Supremacy

I wanted her to feel a lot of pain and not enjoy none of it. The more pain
she felt, the higher I felt. . . .
I pulled out of her when I was about to come and I shot in her face
and came all over her. It was like I pulled a gun and blew her brains out.
That was my fantasy. . . .[26]

The Penalties

The Civil-Rights Antipornography Ordinance has absolutely nothing to
do with police action, a morals squad, or a censorship board; it would
function entirely in the form of complaints and civil suits brought by
individual plaintiffs, not through prosecutions brought by the state. Under
the Ordinance, a plaintiff could not get anyone arrested or put in jail, the
police could not conduct a raid, and there could not be a criminal
prosecution. The justice a plaintiff could get could take these forms,
depending on cause of action:

• Under the coercion provision, a person could sue for money damages from the makers and distributors of the pornography—the product of the coercion—and a person could also sue for a court-ordered
injunction to get the pornography into which the person was coerced
off the market in the place where the Ordinance is law.

• Under the provision about forcing pornography on someone, a person
could sue for money damages from the perpetrator and/or the institution under whose authority the forcing occurred, and for a court-
ordered injunction to stop any further forcing of the pornography on
the plaintiff.

• Under the assault provision, a person could sue the perpetrator of
the assault for money damages; in addition, the assault victim could
sue the makers and sellers of the pornography that was used in the
assault both for money damages and for an injunction against further
sale of it where the Ordinance is in effect.

• Similarly, under the trafficking provision, a person could sue for money damages from the makers, sellers, distributors, and exhibitors and for removal of the pornography from sale in the designated city or area because the pornography is sex discrimination. Under the trafficking provision, a person couldn't sue simply on the basis of isolated passages in something, and any injunction could not be enforced without a full court trial.

Coercion, force, assault, and trafficking are self-evidently not "speech"; they are acts, and they must be proven real before anyone can obtain relief under the Ordinance. The Ordinance requires proof of everything—under standard rules of evidence—including whether there was actual coercion, actual force, actual assault, actual trafficking, and whether the material in question actually meets the statutory definition. The only thing the Ordinance does not require proof of is whether these acts constitute sex discrimination. Essentially, the Ordinance says, if as a matter of fact such-and-such happened, then as a matter of law what happened was sex discrimination.

Enforcement of penalties would be by court order, and anyone found not complying with the order could be found in contempt of court through a separate proceeding. Under the Civil-Rights Antipornography Ordinance, there are no penalties for mere possession of any material, even if it meets the definition of pornography in the Ordinance and even if a court orders an injunction against sale of it.

The Statutory Definition of Pornography

When a case is brought under any of the four causes of action, the plaintiff would have to prove, among other things, that the alleged pornography is in fact pornography as defined in the Ordinance. The statutory definition is a very specific, narrow, and concrete one compared with most definitions in law. It was written based on a thorough study of what is actually made, bought, and sold today; it accurately describes the material actually produced by the ten-billion-dollar-a-year pornography industry. It does not resemble definitions in an obscenity law in any way.

Basically, the Ordinance says, something is pornography if and only if it meets four specific tests. Whether any given material meets the four tests is a matter that must be proved as a finding of fact—by a human-rights commission or a court, in a trial, in an adversarial proceeding; and the burden of proof is on the plaintiff. Rules of evidence would be the same as in any civil proceeding; and depending on how the Ordinance was adopted into local civil-rights law, a judge, a jury, or in some cases the local human-rights commission would decide the factual question. If it cannot be proved that the material meets *all four* tests, then no cause of action involving it can be sustained. The four tests are:

(1) **It must be graphic.** This means, essentially, that it must be unambiguous—not merely implied or suggested.

And:

(2) **It must be sexually explicit.** The words "sexually explicit" are not defined within the Ordinance because accumulated case law has given them a meaning—specific genital acts, sadomasochism, and so forth—that courts have already found to be clear. Hence the Ordinance excludes anything that is merely sexually suggestive or anything in which sexual activity is simply implicit, not explicit and graphically shown.

And:

(3) **It must be the subordination of women.** The word "subordi-nation" is used exactly in its ordinary dictionary meaning: the act of sub-ordinating; the act of placing in a lower order, class, or rank; the act of making subject or subservient, and so forth. (This happens to be a paraphrase of Webster's Third New International, though other diction-aries are pretty similar.) Crucially, the word "subordination" as used in the Ordinance is a noun specifying *an act* (or, as Dworkin and MacK-innon have often called it, a practice). Thus, in order to meet the statu-tory definition of pornography, something may not merely advocate or

express the subordinate status of women; but rather, it must itself actively subordinate women—and there must be proof (in court, in a trial) that it does so.

Because the word "subordination" is unfamiliar in this particular legal context, it has provoked a lot of controversy and confusion; yet the *idea* of subordination has a clear precedent in sex-discrimination law. What is original in the Ordinance is the connection it makes between the harm to a class of people (women) through sex discrimination that takes the particular form of pornography. This unique approach not only defines materials that do harm *on the basis of that harm*; it also defines these materials according to a particular *type* of harm (that is, sex discrimination), and thus it creates a claim under civil-rights law. This legal innovation profoundly distinguishes the civil-rights approach from the history of obscenity litigation in this country, which has never been based on a showing of actual harm to any actual people.

The definition of pornography in the Ordinance is both gender-specific and gender-inclusive. The definition first enumerates what the pornography does according to the ways it uses women, but then a separate clause extends the definition to encompass material that actively subordinates men, children, and transsexuals in the same way that women are subordinated in pornography.

And:

(4) **It must include at least one from a list of specific scenarios listed in the Ordinance**. The Minneapolis version of the law listed nine scenarios. A later version of the Ordinance was passed in Indianapolis that condensed this list to six and focused on more overtly violent pornography. First, here is the Minneapolis version:

a. women are presented dehumanized as sexual objects, things or commodities; or

b. women are presented as sexual objects who enjoy pain or humiliation; or

c. women are presented as sexual objects who experience sexual pleasure in being raped; or

d. women are presented as sexual objects tied up or cut up or mutilated or bruised or physically hurt; or

e. women are presented in postures of sexual submission; or

f. women's body parts—including but not limited to vaginas, breasts, and buttocks—are exhibited, such that women are reduced to those parts; or

g. women are presented as whores by nature; or

h. women are presented being penetrated by objects or animals; or

i. women are presented in scenarios of degradation, injury, abasement, torture, shown as filthy or inferior, bleeding, bruised, or hurt in a context that makes these conditions sexual.[27]

Here is the Indianapolis list of scenarios:

a. women are presented as sexual objects who enjoy pain or humiliation; or

b. women are presented as sexual objects who experience sexual pleasure in being raped; or

c. women are presented as sexual objects tied up or cut up or mutilated or bruised or physically hurt, or as dismembered or truncated or fragmented or severed into body parts; or

d. women are presented being penetrated by objects or animals; or

e. women are presented in scenarios of degradation, injury, abasement, torture, shown as filthy or inferior, bleeding, bruised, or hurt in a context that makes these conditions sexual; [or]

f. women are presented as sexual objects for domination, conquest, violation, exploitation, possession, or use, or through postures or positions of servility or submission or display.

[Note: Material that meets only this sixth criterion would not be actionable under the Indianapolis trafficking provision—an exception that came to be called "the *Playboy* exemption."][28]

Material has to meet all the parts of the statutory definition or else a lawsuit involving it cannot be brought for any reason—not coercion, not forcing it on someone, not assault, and not trafficking. For example, material that is sexually explicit but premised on equality could never fall under this law. The law does not proscribe graphic nudity by itself, graphic sexual explicitness by itself, any particular graphic connection of similar or different genitals, or any material such as sexist advertising that might arguably subordinate women but that is not sexually explicit, or anything else that is not pornography as defined: "the graphic sexually explicit subordination of women."

The Civil-Rights Approach versus Obscenity Law

The statutory definition defines pornography in terms of whom it *harms*—those whom it causes injury to by *putting down*. Obscenity laws do not even mention the word "pornography"; they are criminal laws against *obscenity*, which is often defined in very vague words like "lewd" and "lascivious" (and which case law talks of as "morbid" and "depraved"). The Supreme Court has decided that material is obscene and therefore illegal if it meets the so-called Miller test. One part of this test requires that "the average person, applying contemporary community standards, would find that the work, taken as a whole, appeals to the prurient interest." In effect, this defines obscenity in terms of whom it turns on.

The Civil-Rights Antipornography Ordinance defines pornography that is actionable in terms of injury to victims—either to individual victims or to victims as a class. Obscenity laws, however, are written to outlaw material that offends public morals. A second clause in the Miller test, for instance, defines material as criminally obscene if "the work depicts or describes, in a patently offensive way, sexual conduct specifically defined by the state law." This refers to the fact that many state obscenity laws specifically prohibit depictions of certain sex acts, including any same-sex sex acts.

A third part of the Miller test permits an obscenity ban if "the work, taken as a whole, lacks serious literary, artistic, political, or scientific value." This part of obscenity laws has allowed pornographers to wrap the exploitation and subordination of women inside high-toned intellectual articles and peddle the product for astronomical profit.

Obscenity laws are inherently subjective and arbitrary in their application because they criminalize a notion of indecency that does no real harm. There's no evidence that obscenity causes any harm. But there's a lot of evidence that pornography—as defined in the civil-rights Ordinance—is harmful.

These two lists summarize the differences between the use of a civil-rights approach to confront pornography and the use of obscenity law.

CIVIL-RIGHTS APPROACH	OBSCENITY LAW
A civil law	A criminal law
Complaint or lawsuit initiated by plaintiff with a cause of action	State prosecution triggered by police officer with a perception of moral offense
Adjudicated by human-rights commission or tried in civil court	Tried in criminal court
Remedies for violated civil rights: money damages and/or injunction	Punishment for violation of statute: imprisonment, fine, censorship
Pornography defined according to harm	Obscenity defined by arousal
Claim based on injury to victim	Crime based on offense to public morals
Class injury: subordination	Community offense: "indecency"

The Civil-Rights Antipornography Ordinance was drafted to address this central harm: the subordination of women. The radical-feminist understanding that women are subordinated, in part, through sex itself is pivotal to the understanding that developed this Ordinance, although it specifically does not address private behavior—it addresses only the subordination of women that is tied to the production, distribution, sale, and consumption of pornography.

Ironically, the emergence of the Civil-Rights Antipornography Ordinance has brought out of the closet unusually widespread support for obscenity laws. Decisions written on it so far by both district- and appeals-court judges have cited obscenity laws reverentially, of course. But even outside the judiciary, everyone from the pornographers to their ACLU front people now seems to think obscenity laws are just dandy. The pornographers routinely budget legal defense as a cost of doing business, a few of their lawyers get hefty fees, not much stuff ever gets prosecuted because the laws don't work very well anymore, even less gets taken off the market, organized crime continues to profit from pornography enormously, and no one who's actually hurt has any rights to recover diddly squat.

In fact the most cogent legal and political critique of obscenity laws today is coming from radical-feminist antipornography activists. Most notably, for instance, Andrea Dworkin has argued vehemently against obscenity laws for five specific reasons: [29]

1. Obscenity laws have become the formula for making pornography. According to present law, so long as the tortured bodies of women are marketed in a socially redeeming wrapper—some literary, artistic, political, or scientific value—it doesn't matter what the pornographers do to women.

2. The prurient-interest test of obscenity is irrelevant to the reality of what is happening to women in pornography. In fact, this test has probably contributed to the production of more and more sadistic pornography, since the more repulsive the material, the less likely a jury would be to

believe that an average person would find it sexually arousing. Moreover, the Supreme Court has recently "clarified" the prurient-interest test by taking two synonyms, "lust" and "lasciviousness," and saying that they mean different things, which now means that this criterion is even more meaningless and mind-boggling.

3. The community-standards test is also irrelevant to what pornography does to women. What do community standards mean in a society where violence against women is virtually the norm, where battery is the most commonly committed violent crime, where fewer than one out of every ten women ever makes it through her lifetime unharassed and unassaulted sexually?[30] For that matter, what do community standards mean given the power of pornography to change how much violence and callousness toward women that people will condone, a power that social-science research has demonstrated time and time again? And as Dworkin says, "What would community standards have meant in the segregated South? What would community standards have meant as we approached the atrocity of Nazi Germany? What are community standards in a society where women are persecuted for being women and pornography is a form of political persecution?"[31]

4. Obscenity laws are completely inadequate to the reality of today's technology. They were drafted in an age when obscenity was construed to be essentially writing and drawing, but now there is the mass production and consumption of real photographic documentations of real people being hurt. Meanwhile obscenity laws are constructed on the presumption that it is women's bodies that are dirty, that women's bodies are the filth, which is also a major pornographic theme and which completely misses the point of what happens to real women in and through pornography.

5. Obscenity laws are totally useless for interrupting the bigotry, hostility, aggression, and sexual abuse that pornography creates against women. The only thing obscenity laws have been able to do, at the discretion of police and prosecutors, is occasionally to keep a few items

out of the public view. But these laws have had virtually no effect on the availability of pornography to men in private, to individual men, to all-male groups. Pornography is still used in private as part of sexual abuse. The pornography itself is still produced through blackmail, through coercion, through exploitation; and the pornography industry is thriving, making more and more money over more and more women's dead or near-dead bodies.

The Legislative and Judicial Progress of the Ordinance

The original Civil-Rights Antipornography Ordinance as authored by Dworkin and MacKinnon was passed by the Minneapolis City Council for the first time December 30, 1983.

Needless to say, what happened in Minneapolis became a national astonishment. Shock waves went out. Many allegedly progressive people had a basic problem with the Ordinance: It took a stand against eroticized domination and subordination; it took a stand against male-supremacist sex; it took a stand against the very sexual conduct that makes injustice feel sexy. There was a rather widespread horror at the notion that a woman, a mere woman, might ever enter a courtroom and possibly prove—through cumbersome and expensive litigation—that a particular manifestation of male-supremacist sex had injured her and that her injury had specifically to do with the fact that she was a woman. The new law would let a woman prove that a particular instance of male-supremacist sex had done what male-supremacist sex is after all *supposed* to do: make her inferior and harm her, make her subordinate, make her suffer the sexual freedom of men. So it became a question of community standards, of how much justice a city could tolerate.

Opponents raised an issue of freedom of speech that was really an issue about freedom of sex. Their argument was really an argument for the sexuality that feels its freedom most exquisitely when it is negating someone else's freedom. It was about wanting to keep safe the style of sexual subordination to which they had become accustomed, the sexual freedom that abhors sexual justice, the sexuality that can get hard and come only when it is oblivious to another person's human rights. And it was an argument to keep off the public record any acknowledgement that male-supremacist sex is dangerous, especially to women.

Perhaps most profoundly, the antipornography Ordinance would help make victims *conscious* of their civil rights. The existence of the Ordinance would have an important effect symbolically in terms of helping carve out social consciousness about what equal rights for women really must mean. Just as the existence of laws against marital rape has a "ripple effect" on people's minds—sending out the message that women are not to be raped in marriage, even to those who don't use the laws against it—this Ordinance would be a community's declaration that women have civil rights that pornography may not trample on. And that would have a radical effect: That would shake male supremacy to its core—because the pleasure of subordinating a woman sexually depends on men's social certainty that she is civilly if not physically powerless to fight back. But if she *can* genuinely fight back and get justice, the subordination stops feeling so sexy.

On January 5, 1984, the Ordinance was vetoed by Mayor Donald M. Fraser—an ostensibly liberal and progressive politician who is active in Amnesty International protesting political torture *abroad*. He said the Ordinance abridged the First Amendment.

The bill was passed again by a newly elected city council in July 1984, and again the mayor vetoed it, this time because he said it would be too expensive to defend in the courts against a suit that the ACLU had promised to bring if the city passed the law. At the same time that he vetoed the civil-rights antipornography bill, he signed a new criminal obscenity law, which was more misogynistic and homophobic than the law it was replacing, and which the ACLU voiced no objection to. He also signed a criminal law requiring opaque covers on pornography. In

Minneapolis, both city councils that passed the Ordinance were primarily liberal; the second city council was almost entirely Democratic.

Meanwhile, a slightly modified version of the law—with the definition of pornography narrowed to focus only on overtly violent pornography—was passed by the Indianapolis City Council in April 1984. Indianapolis mayor William H. Hudnut III readily signed it into law, but he and the city were sued within an hour by a group called the Media Coalition, an alliance of trade groups including booksellers and video sellers and magazine distributors, with backing from the ACLU. Unfortunately the City of Indianapolis was sued for passing this law before any person could file a complaint under it, because enforcement was enjoined, again on First Amendment grounds. This meant that the Media Coalition suit was a "paper challenge," and the district court was asked to judge the law without a real case of a real human being alleging that her civil rights have been injured and trying to use the law to get some justice. In November 1984, District Court Judge Sarah Evans Barker issued her opinion that the Ordinance was unconstitutional. The Ordinance, as she acknowledged, poses a constitutional conflict "between the First Amendment guarantees of free speech, on the one hand, and the Fourteenth Amendment right to be free from sex-based discrimination, on the other hand."[32] But Judge Barker, a Reagan appointee, decided that sex-discrimination interests never outweigh First Amendment interests—despite Supreme Court rulings to the contrary.[33] Barker's decision was full of naïve peculiarities, such as this: "Adult women generally have the capacity to protect themselves from participating in and being personally victimized by pornography"—and therefore, she argued, "the State's interest in safeguarding the psychological well-being of women . . . [is] not so compelling as to sacrifice the guarantees of the First Amendment."[34] Also, Judge Barker's decision seemed not to be based on any familiarity with very much pornography itself. Take, for example the pictures in the December 1984 *Penthouse* showing Asian women hung from trees, tied up in bundles like heaps of dead flesh, with rough hemp

Pornography and Male Supremacy

ropes bound through their bare genitals, their faces hidden behind masks. *Penthouse* publisher Bob Guccione, in a letter to *The New York Times*, defended those pictures as "cultural illustration." [35] But it was real action that produced these pictures. Real things were done to real women. The women had to be abused to get the pictures of women being abused. According to Guccione, they are mere illustrations. According to Judge Barker, there is only speech there: protected speech and no lack of freedom. Apparently, one can do anything one wants to women so long as there's a photographer taking pictures and so long as one owns the means to sell those pictures far and wide.

Vowing to take the Ordinance all the way to the Supreme Court, the City of Indianapolis next appealed Judge Barker's ruling to the Seventh U.S. Circuit Court of Appeals in Chicago. The decision written for that court by Judge Frank Esterbrook acknowledged that pornography does "perpetuate subordination" of women and that "[t]he subordinate status of women in turn leads to affront and lower pay at work, insult and injury at home, battery and rape on the streets." However, Esterbrook, like Barker a Reagan appointee, declared that "this simply demonstrates the power of pornography as speech" and therefore, because this harm to women is done through speech, the Constitution protects it.[36]

Appealing finally to the Supreme Court, attorneys for Indianapolis argued:

The legislative record shows that the pornography industry produces verbal and visual sexual entertainment made from coercion, rape, extortion, exploitation, intimidation, fraud and unequal opportunities. This material then engenders coercion, rape, extortion, exploitation, intimidation, fraud and unequal opportunities through its consumption. Pornography, as defined [in the Ordinance], and when coerced, forced on individuals, the cause of assault, or actively trafficked, is inseparable from aggression and terror, crimes, torts, and unspeakable indignities. Although men are also victimized and also covered [by the Ordinance], women and children are [pornography's] primary targets and victims.

Having accepted this reality, each [lower] court ruled that stopping this injustice is not as important to the Constitution as inflicting it. . . . To assign such a low value to women's rights, without weighing them against this means of sex-specific victimization, is to legitimize sex inequality.[37]

Finally, in February 1986, the Supreme Court voted six to three not to hear oral arguments in the case and affirmed Judge Esterbrook's appeals-court decision, which had said, in effect, that a legislative exception to the First Amendment cannot be made based on a showing of social harm—at least to women—which is simply not true as a matter of law. By affirming this broad appeals-court ruling, the Supreme Court effectively shielded the harms done to women by pornographers in a way that could seriously undercut many other legal efforts to balance the rights of injured parties against those who are doing the injury in part through speech—such as anti-Klan work. Because Esterbrook's ruling was at pains to reach back into history and provide a sweeping First Amendment protection for even "Hitler's orations[, which] affected how some Germans saw Jews,"[38] some in the radical-feminist antipornography movement called it "a progenocide decision."

Catharine A. MacKinnon, a coauthor of the Indianapolis Ordinance, said that the Supreme Court vote to affirm Esterbrook's decision shows "women's rights are a joke."[39] And coauthor Andrea Dworkin called the decision outrageous: "It shows that the legal system protects the pornography industry and anything that the pornography system does to women is all right. . . . I don't understand how it is that a woman being cut up with knives is an expression of a point of view that gets First Amendment protection."[40]

The Ordinance and the First Amendment

The particular legal and moral issue being raised about pornography today by radical feminists is about how pornography in particular works, what pornography in particular does, and the particular way that in pornography speech and action are meshed.

The issues being raised about pornography by radical feminists are legally and politically original—they are completely different, for instance, from social-purity crusades. The issue of pornography, as raised by radical feminists, turns on whether pornographers should be able to hide behind claimed First Amendment rights in order to promote hostility, bigotry, aggression, and assault against individual women and women as a class.

Casting the issue this way results in social-policy questions such as these:

• How much abuse should the First Amendment shield?

• To what extent does the First Amendment immunize sexual exploitation?

• To what extent is the state's ostensible interest in ending sex discrimination compatible with the pornographer's economic incentive to perpetuate it?

• Does the Fourteenth Amendment's guarantee of equal protection apply to women who are injured in or through pornography?

• If harm is done in part through speech—if there is, for instance, an injury to an individual in the production of the so-called speech, or if something called speech is used to hurt someone thousands and thousands of times over—does the fact that speech is involved mean that the injury may not be redressed?

There are already many existing exceptions to First Amendment protections because certain forms of expression cause harm, especially harm that cannot be redressed or undone by more speech:

• Child pornography, because of a recent Supreme Court decision, is criminally banned. (Both the Media Coalition and the ACLU, incidentally, opposed any law against child pornography, arguing that it must be protected speech.)

• Obscenity, legally, is not even considered speech—even though it exists in words and pictures.

168

- Libel and group libel are still prohibited, even though there is much confusion about how the laws should be applied and interpreted.
- "Fighting words" are not protected—for instance, a person cannot walk up to you on the street and call you a "fascist," because the presumption is that the insult will provoke violence, and therefore it is not protected.
- Incitement to violence is not protected.
- Blackmail and bribery are crimes done through words that do not have First Amendment protection.

The harm of pornography is not identical to the harm caused by any of these unprotected types of speech, yet there are many similarities in how these exceptions have been argued legally. But because women have been systematically excluded from human-rights considerations, there is not yet a clear-cut precedent for legal arguments for new law that addresses the effects of pornography on women: civil inferiority and sexual abuse. That's why a major part of the effort to pass the Civil-Rights Antipornography Ordinance is to bring into the legal system feminist legal arguments that take the reality of women's lives seriously.

There is a more radical First Amendment issue that the Civil-Rights Antipornography Ordinance brings up as well. The First Amendment protects *those who have already spoken* from state interference. But women and blacks, in particular, have been systematically excluded from public discourse by civil inferiority, economic powerlessness, and violence. Right now, the First Amendment protects those who can buy communication and allows them to use communication as a club against the powerless.

Pornography—the making, the selling, and the use of it—often silences women and makes women afraid to stand up for their rights as equal human beings; meanwhile the rich pornography industry spends millions of dollars on lawyers to protect its right to keep saying to women, in effect: "You are nothing but a whore and men should be able to do anything they want to you."

The First Amendment can be a bulwark of freedom only when it is used and understood and honored in conjunction with rights of equality, in particular the principles underlying the Fourteenth Amendment, which guarantees equal protection under law. One of the main reasons there needs to be this Civil-Rights Antipornography Ordinance is that sexual abuse and civil worthlessness silence women—and in order to have democratic discourse, one must have women's speech.

Strangely, one hears some of the most dire warnings about how this Ordinance could be abused from people in the progressive legal community, those same folks who, under virtually every other circumstance of injustice, look to every possible innovative application of the law for redressing actual harm to actual individuals. But in the case of pornography, they seem to want to make an exception a mile wide. "No," this progressive legal community seems to say, "the harm done by pornography ought not be redressed through any conceivable application of the law." On the issue of pornography, there exists an apparent convergence of legal opinion, from "liberal" to "conservative," to the effect that the law can only "protect" if it is protecting the rights of the exploiters. Even more astonishing is all these lawyers' apparent failure even to imagine that the law might weigh and balance the rights of the exploiters and the rights of the harmed. Their implicit distrust in the law as an instrument of effecting justice here is truly staggering.

What the Civil-Rights Approach Would Achieve

The Ordinance would definitely hurt the pornography industry. Pornographers could not operate with impunity anymore. They would be hurt economically; they would be at risk legally; and they would be hurt in their social legitimacy, which they very much want. Economically, the Ordinance would, as its drafters have suggested, "take the profit motive out of rape." The threat of civil liability would be an economic disincentive to actively subordinate women through the production and distribution of materials that do that. Also, through the use of discovery motions in civil trials, information about pornographers' financial dealings and other matters could be obtained. This information could be used, as Dworkin has suggested,[41] to develop prosecutions against organized-crime involvement in the industry.

But just as significantly, the Ordinance would empower victims; it would empower the exploited to fight back against the exploiters.

This would be a feminist law, designed to bring the feminist analysis of women's inequality through sexual exploitation into the center of public policy and constitutional jurisprudence. This is a law that would increase civil liberties—extend the right of speech to many who are now part of a silent, powerless victim class—people who have been hurt and who have no legal way to fight back for justice.

And essentially, this would be an equality law, because it would attack sex inequality and the civil inferiority of women head on: by demanding human rights for women, by demanding human dignity for women, by demanding an end to the buying and selling of women's bodies and sexuality and an end to the profit from sexual abuse that is presented as entertainment.

Part IV

Activism and Moral Selfhood

Feminist Activism and Male Sexual Identity

For a panel about what direction "the men's movement"
should take

At issue: reproductive freedom.

Pregnant poor women,
    denied dignity,
    denied integrity,
    denied a safe home.
Now their lives hang in the balance
    against a gob of cells.
Now the superfathers of America say
    that gob of cells deserves more dignity,
    that gob of cells has more integrity,
    that gob of cells has a paramount right to a safe home.

Pregnant teenagers, children bearing children,
    one million every year.
Now the superfathers of America say, "Stay chaste or else."
Now the superfathers of America say,
    "The paramount right to life resides in your uterus,
        not in you."
Now the superfathers of America say,
    "Go knock up your daughters,
        your stepdaughters,
        your nieces,
    go on;
    that gob of cells has a paramount right to life."

As if there was a question
    what men of conscience should do.

        At issue: rape.

Penetration on demand.
Penises engorged with rage.
Tender, vulnerable organ—
    with a little help it gets hard.
    With a little help from fists,
        knives,
        force,
        contempt.
    With a little help from friends:
        two on one,
        three on one,
        ten on one . . .

Tender, vulnerable organs all wanting
                              in,
               all wanting
                         fun.
Penetration on demand.
Surefire fail-safe proof the guy's a man.

As if there was a question
what men of conscience should do.

~~At issue: marital rape.~~

The right to rape that comes with the wedding cake.
          His conjugal right.
          Her connubial duty.
          Whenever he gets hungry,
                    he gets his piece of cake.
          Lip-smacking good.
She's his.
          His piece.
Can't say no now.
          Can't ever say no.
She said a permanent yes to one penis forever.
          Forever is a long time.
          Forever is anytime.

Now the legislators of America know a good thing
          when they see one. Now they see couples by the millions
          just shacking up, not getting a license,
          living outside the sacred bondage.
          No matter, say the legislators. They're passing

laws across the land to make the right to rape
legal in cohabitation,
to make the right to rape legal
if she ever said yes once—
                yes once on a date,
                yes once three years ago,
                yes once just once:
a yes to any penis is permanent,
                say these clever new laws.
Extend the marriage contract to the unmarried,
                                to the roommates,
                                to the date.
Skip the cake.
Get down to the business of devouring female lives.

As if there was a question
        what men of conscience should do.

                At issue: battery.

She walked into a door.
She fell down some stairs doing the laundry.
Her dark glasses are prescription.
She limps from a slight sprain.
She went to the hospital to visit a friend.
Her screaming was all in fun,
        it was laughing,
        hysterical laughing,
        you know how women are.

Fashions change.
The look today is abused.

Clothing that looks slit by a knife.
Faces made up like flesh bruised from beating.
Around the haunted, deep-set eyes:
    black and blue.
On the temples and cheekbones:
    purplish-magenta welts,
    brushed on or beaten on,
    in a patch the size of a fist,
    broken blood vessels pancaked over.
It takes a lot of pancake to cover damaged goods.

Check out the street.
The abused look is in.

Men like their women beautiful.
They see beauty in women's pain.

Go to your corner drugstore,
    check it out,
    Get your personal bruise kit
    in the latest, chic-est shades.
Or just go home.

The beauty of pain is within the reach
    of every woman
    within a man's reach.

As if there was a question
    what men of conscience should do.

At issue: child sexual assault.

They calculate the age at which
    the diameter of a child's vagina

---

can accommodate a grown man's penis.
They think it's eight.
Or
they don't bother to calculate.
The infants go to the hospital
        with gonorrhea down their throats.

They pick up children and drug them.
When the children are passed out,
        they get it on.
Or
they pick up children and keep them conscious.
They photograph them—being pissed on,
                perhaps, or
                spread open,
                poor and pimply,
                in Polaroid.

They pressure their daughters and nieces
        and stepdaughters and little sisters
        into secret sexual intimacies.
Simon says diddle diddle dumpling,
        little miss muffin,
Simon says red rover red rover
        wants to come over and over.
And
they make the girls promise not to tell.
The girls keep the promise:
They grow up unable to speak.

As if there was a question
        what men of conscience should do.

Feminist Activism and Male Sexual Identity

At issue: pornography.

The ropes cutting into her breasts
        give him pleasure.
The gag stuffed into her mouth
        makes him feel full to bursting.
The black leather hood over her face
        makes him feel radiant,
        hot.
The chains around her ankles and wrists
        make him feel strong,
        like an ox ready to gore.
The pincers ripping her nipples
        make his penis swell.
The way she spreads her labia
        makes him feel like fucking her
        raw.

He imagines her.
He has her.
He uses her.
He possesses her.

As if there was a question
        what men of conscience should do.

What Men of Conscience Will Be Doing in the Next Decade

PREDICTION: Many men of conscience will do very little or nothing.

PREDICTION: Many men of conscience will prefer to discuss their feelings.

PREDICTION: Many men of conscience will do only that which makes them feel better about themselves. If something does not make them feel better about themselves, they will be unlikely to do it. Discussing their feelings will make them feel better about themselves.

PREDICTION: Many men of conscience, if they notice they are doing nothing, will want to spend hours and hours struggling with the question of what is politically correct for them to do *as men*. *As men*: the two most paralyzing words in the vocabulary of the so-called man of conscience. He won't do anything until it is clear to him how it affects him and his brethren *as men*. He won't do anything unless it is clear to him in what sense he can do it with other men *as men*, unless their action particularly matters because they are doing it *as men*, unless the action makes them all feel much better about themselves *as men*. *As men*. Words to live by. Words to do nothing by.

PREDICTION: Many men of conscience, if they notice they are doing nothing, will want to spend hours and hours justifying their inertia. They are waiting for women's leadership, they may say. They don't want to do anything rash; they want it all spelled out for them exactly, step-by-step. And they have not yet received precise instructions from the central feminist organizing committee. All women have to do is ask, they may say. All women have to do is hold their hand, is what they mean.

PREDICTION: Many men of conscience will spend more time shopping for tofu than they spend reading the feminist press.

PREDICTION: Many men of conscience will turn out for one feminist demonstration every twelve months. They will raise their voices in shout. They will shout louder, in fact, than all the women combined. They will even get into a scuffle with some other men, any other men, hostile bystanders, the police: They will make a noble scene; they will stage a cockfight. Then they will go home and try to get in touch with their feelings for another year.

PREDICTION: Many men of conscience will ally themselves publicly with a woman of feminist credentials. They may be friends or lovers,

heterosexual or homosexual, married or single, living together or apart—
it doesn't matter; what matters is their public alliance. She will provide
him with credentials of his own: a plastic-laminated wallet card that says
"I have been approved by a feminist woman" and it will have on it her
good name. He will flash the card when it suits him. He will keep it in
his pocket when he buys pornography. When he visits her home he will
leave a mess.

PREDICTION: Many men of conscience, when their wife says goodbye, when their live-in maid says clean your own piss around the toilet,
when their politically astute feminist comrade-in-arms says "I no longer
trust you" and stops wanting to hang out together—when their personal
conduit to feminist consciousness leaves them—many men of conscience
will become less and less like men of conscience and more and more
like ordinary men. They will turn their attention to political issues that
don't blatantly remind them of the fact that men like themselves oppress
women like her. Nuclear energy. Wars in foreign lands. Food co-ops.
Rent strikes. Important issues, not unimportant issues. It's just that they're
better than alcohol or drugs when your heart is broken and you want it
to harden.

Some Questions Often Asked about Feminist Activism and Male Sexual Identity

QUESTION: If it's true that men are the doers, the agents of history,
the performers, the active ones, how come men are so passive?

QUESTION: Can a man have a feminist consciousness if he doesn't
consistently act on it?

QUESTION: Can high consciousness exist in a man who is more or
less inert? How high can consciousness go before the fact that it exists in
a lump becomes a political embarrassment to the lump?

QUESTION: Is there a way to seem to be a man of fine feminist manners when you're trying to impress people to whom it matters while at the same time keeping open your options to hob-nob with woman-haters?

QUESTION: Which of the following is the most convincing pretext for not doing anything about sexist injustice: (a) self-hatred, (b) guilt, (c) more pressing political priorities, or (d) "Can't you see I'm trying?" Are some women more taken in by some pretexts than by others? How can I tell the difference? Where can I meet the women who are easy?

QUESTION: If men are so evil, what's the use?

ANSWER: Was that pretext (e)?

QUESTION: Don't we first have to work out some serious and personal questions about when and how and whether we're going to have sex?—I mean, what's in this for me and my penis?

QUESTION: What happens when a man takes feminism utterly seriously, in every area of his life, in every moment of everything he does? Does he still stay a man?—or does he turn into something else?

QUESTION: Why is it so difficult to hold on to my sense of maleness in the company of women? Why does being in large groups of mostly women protesting sexist injustice make me feel like shit? Why do I need a gaggle of men around me to feel better? Why is it so difficult to get a gaggle of men to clear their calendars so they can gather around me and help me feel better? Does penis size matter? Am I getting off the subject? What is the subject?

ANSWER: Feminist activism and male sexual identity.

QUESTION: How can I always know I am male and not female and not in between, how can I always know I belong to the male sex and not the other one, how can I always want there to be a male sex to belong to, how can I know it's always okay to belong to it, how can I always feel good about myself as a man and feel truly male at the same time, how can I always enjoy the company of other men? How do you expect me to identify with women's struggle for justice? Don't you see that my aloofness is politically necessary? Don't you see that gender injustice is necessary so I can feel good as a man? Don't you see that sexism is necessary so I can have a sex?

Some Closing Thoughts

Male sexual identity is not a "role."

Male sexual identity is not a set of anatomical traits.

Male sexual identity—the belief that one is male, the belief that there is a male sex, the belief that one belongs to it—is a politically constructed idea.

This means that masculinity is an ethical construction: We construct it through our acts, through the things we choose to do and not do, through the acts we commit that are "male" things to do. Most of our choice making has to do with choosing to do acts that will make the idea of our maleness real and that will keep far away the idea that, really, this dividing up of the species into two separate and distinct sex classes may be utterly specious after all. Most of our choice making has to do with dissociating from all that is coded and stigmatized "female." Most of our choice making has to do with disidentifying with women. Most of our choice making creates our sexedness.

So long as we continue to try to act in ways that keep us still "men," we are doomed to paralysis, guilt, self-hatred, inertia. So long as we try to act *as men*, in order to continue to *be* men, in order to do our bit in the social construction of the entity that is the *sex class* men, we doom women to injustice: the injustice that inheres in the very idea that there are two sexes.

Male sexual identity is constructed through the choices we make and the actions we take. We cannot continue to construct it and give ourselves fully to feminist activism. One cannot cling to one's gender as the core of one's being and be of use in the struggle. One must change the core of one's being. The core of one's being must love justice more than manhood.

Other Men

Some of us are the other men that some of us are very wary of. Some of us are the other men that some of us don't trust. Yet some of us are the other men that some of us want to be close to and hang out with. Some of us are the other men that some of us long to embrace.

The world of other men is a world in which we live behind a barrier—because we need to for safety, because we understand there is something about other men that we know we have to protect ourselves from. The world of other men is also a world in which we know we are sized up by other men and judged by other men and sometimes threatened by other men. The world of other men can be, we know, a scary and dangerous place.

I have been obsessed with other men for a long, long time. I have lived years of my life agonizing about how different I felt from other men. I have wanted more than anything to be more like other men than I could ever hope to be. At the same time I have harbored a terror of other men: afraid that they would see through my attempts to act like a man, afraid that I would not measure up, not fit in, not be right. Many of the men I talk with are also in various ways obsessed with other men. We don't talk about it readily; we don't really have the vocabulary for it. But always the issue is there, within us and between us—the issue of how one identifies oneself in relation to other men, the kinds of accommodations and compensations one makes depending on how one rates oneself on some imaginary scale of masculinity: If you think you rate relatively high, or if you think you rate relatively low, you make certain choices in your life, you choose the best deal you can get with the quantity of maleness you feel you can muster. And always other men are the measure of the man you try to be.

As individuals and as a profeminist men's movement, we need to understand what this issue is—why the issue is what it is—and how to think about the issue so that we can do something about it in our lives.

What the Issue Is

One of the reasons I started to care about radical feminism as much as I did was because it seemed to resolve for me a certain dilemma about myself in relation to other men. I had always felt irremediably different—even when no one else noticed, I knew; I knew I wasn't really one of them. When I first began to come in contact with the ideas of radical feminism, those ideas seemed to put to rest that certain trouble. Radical feminism helped me imagine a gender-just future, a notion of a possibility that men need not be brutish and loutish, that women need not be cutesy and coy. It was a vision that energized me. It helped me view the whole male-supremacist structure of gender as a social construction, not as a final judgment on our natures—and not as a final judgment on mine.

Radical feminism helped me honor in myself the differences that I felt between myself and other men; radical feminism helped me know my connections to the lives of women, with whom I had not imagined I would ever find a model for who I could be. And it's also true—and not easy to admit—that radical feminism helped provide me with a form in which to express my anger at other men—an anger that in men can run very deep, as many of us know. I think that for many men who have become antisexists over the past several years, their antisexism has had meaning to them for similar reasons. In various ways, feminism has blown like a gust of fresh air through a lifetime spent agonizing and anguishing about the place of other men in our lives. For a few of us, feminism has helped us breathe a bit easier.

But it would be a mistake to suggest that a man's antisexism puts to rest his ambivalence toward other men. I think that an antisexist consciousness actually makes the conflict more acute. Such a man perceives even more clearly the behaviors and attitudes in other men that he rejects, and he understands more about what those behaviors and attitudes mean, and in a sense they are the behaviors and attitudes in himself that he wants to be rid of, and somehow other men can remind him of the parts of himself that have not changed very much at all, and whereas he briefly felt good about being different from other men, a part of him no longer feels quite different enough. So his anger at other men intensifies, as a means of keeping clear to himself that he's an exception. Meanwhile he misses the company of other men—their ease, their companionship, the good feelings he remembers having had in their presence.

For many men, the issue of other men is a classic conflict of approach and avoidance. For a man whose life increasingly has to do with antisexism, the conflict cuts to the bone. He struggles with what it means to be a man—and whether he feels ashamed or proud.

For antisexist men who are gay, this conflict has an explicitly sexual aspect. The more sensitive a man becomes to the sexism in other men's attitudes and behaviors, the more it matters to him that his sexual partners be men who share his world view, and the less able he is to accept sexist small talk and jokes as a token of the kind of comradeship that he seeks. For a man to whom the sexual-political character of his sexual partners matters, he is increasingly faced with a choice between abandoning his principles and abandoning his sex life. A man of good character is hard to find, as anyone who has looked can tell you.

But whether or not a man longs for a companionship with other men that wants to be sexual, he is confronted with a seemingly insoluble dilemma: He has his ideas, his beliefs, his vision, his commitments, about a just future in which gender would not divide us; and he has a longing for the company and validation of other men—men who, more often than not, do not share his antisexism.

Many of us have lost male friends over our antisexist politics—for the simple and terribly complex ⁻⁻ ₒn that we just could not abide a friend's sexism anymore. There seem to be two untenable options: affiliation and assimilation with men, just falling in with men on men's terms; or separation and estrangement, self-defined isolation. Neither option seems to hold out any long-term promise or possibility; at least to my knowledge, neither really works. You can't hang out all the time with men who are not working at being antisexist and feel good about yourself—it just doesn't work. And you can't feel good about yourself cutting yourself off from other men; that kind of separation becomes what you do and all that you do; who you are becomes a person who is estranged from other men to no purpose. No wonder so many of us are drawn to a notion of a brotherhood that is oblivious to women—a brotherhood that would make it easier to enjoy being a man because you wouldn't ever have to take women's lives seriously—you wouldn't ever have to take seriously what men have done to women because you would live in a world entirely circumscribed by other men, who are all that really matter. That is, after all, what most men seem to enjoy most about being men: They're not women, and they know they don't ever have to really pay any attention to women's lives.

Other Men

Many of us have come to expect so much isolation from other men that even the prospect of cooperating and organizing with other antisexist men for change can make us really wonder, "How do I know these men are any different? How do I know their values are not just the same as other men's? And how do I know, once I fall in with them, that I'll be any different?" For many of us our feminism is virtually synonymous with isolation from other men. And our isolation becomes so debilitating that it stops us from doing anything about our antisexist beliefs. One example: In the past few years there have been a few men—very few, but some here and there in this country and others—who have recognized in pornography the very values that infuse men's social and personal power over women, a structure of eroticized male supremacy and woman hating. The recognition has been a difficult one; and some of those men have in fact cried over it—not sentimental, self-indulgent tears but tears of terrible, dreadful grief over man's inhumanity to woman. And these few men have recognized how much pornography imitates and helps create a power relation in sex between men and women of dominance and submission. They see that what most of pornography teaches, what it shows, what it extols, is like a handbook for most men—a manual of ways to view women, ways to feel about themselves, ways to keep dominance and submission most people's basic idea of what is "sexy." The dominance-and-submission model of sex, a few men have come to see, is the dark heart of dominance and submission in the world. And what have these men done about this recognition? Well, there have been actions, pickets, letters written, support given to the movement of radical-feminist women who are slowly but surely educating people about the model of dominance and submission in pornography and how these are the very values upon which is built the whole sexist superstructure—but the fact is that this recognition comes to men too often in isolation, and the isolation itself is paralyzing.

We have a vision of a world of gender justice, and we want male friends and allies who can enter that world too. We want male friends who respect our women friends. We want male friends with whom we don't have to censor out our political commitments in order to have a conversation. We want male friends who are also helping to create that world. We want male friends who will help get us there. Yet the fact is that each of us is just one man away from selling out our antisexism. All it takes is one situation with another man—a situation that will be different for each of us—a particular man whose company and esteem and companionship we most want, and we will sell out our convictions for that connection; we won't speak our beliefs in order to bond.

Why the Issue Is What It Is

Our antisexism, it's important to remember, has its roots in feminism, which arises out of a sex-class analysis. This sex-class analysis that stands behind us is about men's domination of women and others; it's about how that structure is cultural, not biological, and why that structure can change; it's about how men are not by nature who they are in the world, yet they are in the world as those men; it's about how the sex-class system is male supremacist and why it's got to go; it's about both the possibility and the responsibility for making the world a different place.

How do we know that change is really possible? One important answer to that question is contained in a passage from the book *Our Blood* by Andrea Dworkin, where she makes this crucial distinction between reality and truth:

Reality is *social*; reality is whatever people at a given time believe it to be. . . . Reality is always a function of politics in general and sexual politics in particular—that is, it serves the powerful by fortifying and justifying their right to domination over the powerless. Reality is whatever premises social and cultural institutions are built on. . . . Reality is enforced by those whom it serves so that it appears to be self-evident. Reality is self-perpetuating, in that the cultural and social institutions built on its premises also embody and enforce those premises. . . . The given reality is, of course, that there are two sexes, male and female; that these two sexes are opposite from each other, polar; that the male is inherently positive and the female inherently negative; and that the positive and negative poles of human existence unite naturally into a harmonious whole.

Truth, on the other hand, is not nearly so accessible as reality. . . . Truth is absolute in that it does exist and . . . it is the human project to find it so that reality can be based on it.

I have made this distinction between truth and reality in order to enable me to say something very simple: that while *the system of gender polarity is real, it is not true.* It is not true that there are two sexes which are discrete and opposite, which are polar, which unite naturally and self-evidently into a harmonious whole. . . . The system based on this polar model of existence is absolutely real; but the model itself is not true. We are living imprisoned inside a pernicious delusion, a delusion on which all reality as we know it is predicated.[1]

So here we are: men, inside a male-supremacist system, inside a male-supremacist sex class, inside it as men. What do we do about it? And why is it so difficult and so unthinkable to live as a traitor to that sex class? Why does it touch such a raw nerve to imagine ourselves having just one conversation with another man in which we declare our beliefs and say of his we don't go along when the issue at hand is male supremacy?

Individuals have been known to disavow their allegiance to other kinds of classes without suffering the same identity crisis. For instance, there have been a few children of the rich who have committed their lives to economic justice. Not everything they have done has been exactly the right thing to do, but they have understood that it is wrong that some people are poor and starving and that their own lives can matter and they can do something to make a difference. Despite the fact that their own wealthy families may have sniped at them with scorn, they went ahead and did what they needed to do to create economic justice in the world—and they didn't lose themselves doing it. As a matter of fact, I think many of them would say that they discovered through their activism a sense of themselves that's better than who they were before. In a somewhat analogous way there have been some white people who have understood that to grow up white in this country is to grow up racist, and that either you are doing something and striving through your life to be antiracist or you are racist. It is a choice, and not choosing is to chose to be a racist. Not everything these white people have done to change their own racism and the society's has been exactly the right thing to do, but they did what they did because they understood that racial hate is wrong. As individuals working for racial justice these people met with great animosity from other white people whose race-class interests were being threatened, but these people persevered without losing who they were; on the contrary they *kept* who they were, they kept the best part of who they were.

It is a measure of how much sex class determines "who we fundamentally are" that for us as men to disavow the interests of our sex class makes us feel we disappear. Tangible membership in the sex class men is our primary means to identity. It's a familiar story: You grow up to become a boy and you are terrorized into acting like a boy and you are rewarded for being a boy and you learn to dissociate from your mother by adopting a whole range of fears and hatreds of women and you learn what you need to learn to be accepted into the company of other men. Women shore up this identity; we look to women to affirm this identity. But we get the identity from other men; it is other men we look to as the arbiters of sex-class identity, the identity that gets inside of us, an identity so close to who we think we are that letting go of it scares us to death.

This sex-class construct of identity is not the only possible form in which we can know who we fundamentally are. There is another way that we sometimes do this, and it stems from a part of ourselves that wants fairness and concern and respect between people, a part of ourselves that is very close to our antisexism and our ideals of gender justice. It's that part of ourselves which recoils at sexualized hate. It's that part of ourselves which wants caring and mutuality, both in sex and in the world; it's that part of ourselves which wants to live in a gender-just future already. I'd like to give that part of ourselves a name, and what I'd like to call it is our moral identity. I don't mean moral in the sense of righteous or pure or politically correct; what I mean by moral identity is the part of ourselves that knows the difference between fairness and unfairness, at least in some shadowy way. It's that part of ourselves which is capable of weighing what we see, what we do, what other people do, in terms of some sense we have of what justice should look like. It's a part of ourselves that is capable also of living beyond gender, and it sometimes does. It's also the part of ourselves that is nearest our experience when we are feeling deep remorse and pain over the suffering and injustice that we see in the world.

The sense of ourselves that we get from this moral identity, however, collides inside of us with the identity that we get from our sex class. We have learned that the suffering under male supremacy in the world can cause us great pain to look at—to look at hard; but we have also learned that blocking out of our minds the awareness of how bad things are is easier to do than making things better. So we try to put together a life view that isn't such a bummer. Yet our emergent moral identity whispers, even though its whispers sometimes pitch us into despair and denial.

Which is more real to us: our moral identity or our sex-class identity? Which makes us feel more real? Which gives us back more the feeling of who we want to be? These two constructs of identity are at war inside us. We go in and out of our moral identity, and for each of us there is a pattern of circumstances that makes us go out of it—episodes, for example, of retaliatory anger or laziness. We don't go in and out of our sex-class identity as much. We feel we measure up against it better at times and worse at other times, but in fact we stay in it and we stay in there more than we think. Our sex-class identity is a constant, and we are fundamentally loyal to it. Our moral identity is more ephemeral, and we tend to be only its fair-weather friend. Other men represent to us the crux of this dilemma—other men especially who are at ease in their sex-class identity and status. It's uncomplicated for them; it's complicated for us. We admire their ease, their masculine complacency; at the same time we're angry at them and we don't want to be like them. We experience the dilemma most acutely at those times when we are feeling in a bind between other men and feminism. For instance, an antisexist man's moral identity might respond to the feminist analysis of the sex-class system by wanting to be an exception to it, by not wanting to be like the men the analysis describes, by wanting to make sure he is living in such a way that the analysis isn't true of him in particular. But then his sex-class identity rejects any critique of men as a class, reacts either as if he is the defender of his whole sex class or as if his spectacularly exemplary life redeems it and thus refutes the analysis; his sex-class identity wants to blend in, wants alliances with other men on any terms. His moral identity, on the other hand, recognizes the truth of the sex-class analysis and believes individuals, including himself, can confront male supremacy and transform themselves and the culture; his moral identity recognizes how he is both different from his sex class and yet very much part of it. But his sex-class identity has an overriding vested interest in his identification with the class as a whole.

We can always give up our moral identity in favor of our sex-class identity. It's really quite easy, and it can happen quite without our thinking. For most of us, the issue of other men makes us actually feel an urgency to abandon our moral identity because in order to deal with other men on their terms, that's what we almost always have to do.

Understanding the Issue in Our Lives

So what can we possibly do? How can we sort through this conflicted issue in our lives? In what terms can we possibly understand it so that we might have some clarity about what to do about it both as individuals and as a movement?

First of all, we need to be clear that we're not talking about a market strategy for the profeminist men's movement; we're not talking about how to package the profeminist men's movement so that we can run it up the flagpole and all the men in America will salute. We're also not dealing superficially with some difference between conscience and camaraderie. Nor are we talking about yet another great occasion for navel-gazing—heaven knows we have enough of that.

What this issue really comes down to, I think, is an issue of who we choose to become.

In my view, the discipline of focusing on antisexist activism is really the only way that one can keep choosing to keep one's moral identity alive and awake. I don't believe one's moral identity can survive in an actionless vacuum. It can't just exist in one's mind or in one's statement of principles. It has to be expressed in action.

I don't know the answer to the question "Well, what happens to the sex-class identity we always seem to carry around with us?" But I do know there is a possibility for one's moral identity to shine through one's life more often. As a movement and as individuals, we cannot achieve clarity about our moral identity by evoking a brotherhood that is oblivious, a brotherhood for brotherhood's sake, a brotherhood whose sole purpose becomes the embrace of men simply on account of their being men—like one big sex-class club. To do so does not allow for personal transformation in the struggle to keep and grow your moral identity. The change to which we aspire has got to be predicated on a new integration of selfhood, a radical new identity, a self that knows who it is in relation to reality and who it is in relation to truth. We need a double vision: We need to keep in our mind both the reality of our being men in the sex-class system and the truth of the possibility of a future without it. We need to know, "Yes, as men, we're part of it. And yet we are men who are trying to live differently, trying to make our lives make a difference." We need, I think, as a movement and as individuals, the discipline of action that is transformative of ourselves and society—not simply action that maintains our organization, our own social structures among ourselves. If our antisexist action in the world stops, our moral identity will go into hibernation, and the longer it sleeps, the less it resembles who we could become. As individuals and as a movement, we must not fancy ourselves redeemers of our sex class, as men who will show the world that men are not as bad as some have said—that's a trap laid by a sex-class identity determined to blend back into the comfort of unconscious masculine complacency, determined to forge out of self-congratulation some semblance of self-respect.

The pride to which we aspire is not in being *men* but in being *men who* . . . —men who are living their lives in a way that will make a difference.

We must be transformers of selfhood—our own and others'. If we are not, we will have betrayed women's lives utterly, and we will have lost a part of ourselves that is precious and rare on this earth.

Battery
and the Will to Freedom

An address to a conference on counseling men who batter

It is a great honor to be here. The challenge you have taken on is vital, and I come before you with a mixture of gratitude and deep respect: because you are among the world changers. You are among the transformers of society, from a place where damaged lives are virtually the norm into a place where each life is cherished and each life is fully free. You are helping make the revolution that we can't wait any longer to happen: the revolution to end men's social entitlement to power over and against women.

When a woman is beaten, more breaks than her bones. When a woman lives in fear of yet another abusive outburst, another random act of violence triggered by she doesn't know what next, she lives in a terror that men rarely experience—except as abused children or perhaps political prisoners. When the person she thought she trusted, the person she's trying desperately to love, becomes her private torturer, her personal inquisition, she is wracked with more than pain. What battery does is to beat down a woman's will to freedom. What battery does is to make her think that safety and survival lie in a smaller and smaller life. What battery does is to make her afraid of speaking her own mind, of making any assertion of her human rights. What battery does is to make her so confused, so unable to figure out a logical relationship between the punishment she receives and whatever she did to deserve it, that she loses faith in her own mental faculties. What battery does is to make her believe that she did not love well enough so she has failed as a woman, and to make her so ashamed that her life has come to this that she retreats further and further into shadows and isolation. What battery does is to beat down a woman's will to freedom: because it makes her will to freedom seem her own worst enemy: because she is made to believe that if she expresses it at all, she will only get in more trouble, she will only be more abused.

What battery does is not an easy thing for men to grasp. Most men in our society have no conception of what it means to be deprived of the personal will to freedom.

In this 200th anniversary year of this nation's Constitution, you hear a lot about freedom. Freedom of this, freedom of that. Socially, the freedom that's talked about is white men's freedom. What you don't hear a lot about is the extent to which men's private sexual violence against women has created an underclass of the unfree—an underclass of women who are so unfree that freedom of speech to them is inconceivable: to speak out freely is to risk a particular man's wrath, a particular man's violence, a particular man's silencing. An underclass of women for whom the right of privacy is nonexistent, for whom body access on demand has made both sleep and sex a nightmare. Life, liberty, and the pursuit of happiness do not mean anything if you're being battered.

Most men in this country have a gut knowledge of the difference between freedom and unfreedom. Most men live lives characterized by quite a lot of liberty, actually; but even if they're not relatively free, at least they know it, and they know that freedom is what they need. Most men grew up with a confident sense of their entitlement to freedom, a confidence that was nurtured throughout the exuberance and expansiveness of their youth, a confidence that was congratulated by the culture wherever they turned.

But for some, along the way, an awful message got learned: Your survival as a man depends on conquering the will to freedom of a woman. Defeating it. Making it not exist in your private world, the world you were taught you could own, the world you were taught belonged to you, your home, your castle, where her will to freedom equals your unfreedom, where your freedom equals the extinction of hers: "What are you, anyway, a pussy-whipped wimp? Show her who's boss. Show her whose castle it is."

In this 200th anniversary year of this nation's Constitution, let us note here this morning that millions of women's voices have been silenced, censored by fear and force, within a private sanctuary that our nation defends against *foreign* aggressors—in the bitterly ironic name of "domestic security"—with billions of dollars worth of military might. All that firepower . . . to keep *some* of us safe at home.

You have undertaken, or are about to, the task of working with individual men who have in one way or another attempted to crush the will to freedom of individual women. This makes you, in a sense, freedom fighters. You are using the powers of persuasion and education and counsel and good example to bring a particular man to understand his particular responsibility for what he has done: because you share a rock-hard belief that this responsibility not only *must* be acknowledged, but *can* be acknowledged.

I don't need to tell you: The job is tough.

But what you must always remember is this: The job is revolutionary. The work you are doing, or about to do, is part of a courageous, ongoing struggle to eradicate from humanity all vestiges of male supremacy. That's the big picture. And I want to say something this morning about the absolutely critical role that your work plays in this struggle. To do that I want to focus on how your work can profoundly change the relationship between men's sense of who they are and the responsibility they take for what they do.

Normal masculinity, as I'm sure you're aware, is often tenaciously resistant to acknowledging responsibility of that sort: "She made me do it. I couldn't help myself, she made me so angry. The bitch, she had it coming." You see it in rape too: "She provoked me. She wanted it. *I* didn't do anything wrong." But you also see men's denial and evasion of their responsibility for interpersonal conduct in a whole host of everyday life contexts that apparently (only apparently!) have nothing to do with battery and sexual violence: He bullies her and blames her. Or he lies to her and discounts her. Or he breaks a promise to her and berates her. Normal masculinity, it sometimes seems, is characterologically unable to coexist with a functioning self-awareness of ethical accountability.

This is the big picture too, and it's not pretty.

Manhood is both a developmental process and a normative identity structure. It's not only *how* you grow up, it's *what* you're supposed to grow up to be. It's the pathway and the intended destination. It's the process and the goal.

Too often only the developmental process gets critiqued. In fact, it gets looked to as a sole and sufficient explanation of whatever has gone "wrong"—when a man rapes, when a man batters, when a man sexually violates or humiliates someone for his pleasure. This search for an explanation of men's abusiveness and violence sometimes borders on being a search for an apology: "How could he be any different, poor thing?—look how he grew up!" Thus does men's evasion of ethical accountability get therapeutic validity and academic respectability.

In fact, if you think about it, unconsciousness of ethical accountability is a core component of the masculinity that a lot of men grow up believing they should strive for. Especially in relation to anyone a man perceives as less worthy than himself, less a full person than himself, a real man doesn't have to pay attention to the consequences of his acts. His acts against his "inferiors" don't matter because his inferiors don't matter—and vice versa: The people he thinks are inferior don't matter, so whatever he does to them doesn't matter either.

When we talk about male supremacy—and white supremacy too—one of the things we're really talking about is the ethical abandon with which someone in the socially superior class feels he's entitled to treat someone outside it. The absence of ethical accountability he feels—his lack of regard for how what he does *affects* someone else—is a key fixture of the sexual and racial identity he gets to feel. And it's also the major way that the sex and race class system gets maintained interpersonally.

Among a lot of experts and activists in the antibattery movement, the evidence has generally been accepted that one of the reasons men batter is because of something called "the male sex role stereotype." Now frankly, I don't think those words say enough; they don't go far enough. Those words are not adequate for getting at the ethical core of normative manhood, the place inside a man's head where he knows he's a real man because he gets to believe that someone else is less real—in particular someone who isn't male. Those words "the male sex role stereotype" don't really delineate the way a man's sense of a normal selfhood comes from an ethical transaction, what happens when he actively discounts or damages the selfhood of someone else—in particular someone female. It's a selfhood he doesn't have to be a Rambo to achieve; he just has to put down a woman—to negate her will to freedom.

And if you call him on it, if you say something like, "Look, fella, what you're doing is a real male number," what do you get? Do you get the recognition that you might have a good point there? Do you get the ethical self-reflection of someone who keeps track of what he does and how it might have consequences for someone else? Do you get the moral sensibility of someone who is conscientious about knowing the difference between the right stuff he's done and the wrong stuff he's done, so he'll know as much as he humanly can about how to make his choices better in the future? Do you get a sense of a selfhood that takes full responsibility for its actions, knowing full well that that's really the only way anyone on this earth ever has of honoring their connection to other human life? Is that what you get when you ask normal manhood to take ethical responsibility?

In your counseling work, as you challenge men who have abused women to confront, understand, and own their responsibility for what they have done, you are cracking through—bit by bit—the wall that has been erected between how a man acts toward others and his sense of who he is. Breaking down that wall is crucial. If it stays intact socially, so does the whole superstructure of male supremacy. If it stays intact personally, he'll never know his own connection to the very humanity he so far fails to recognize in the people he thinks don't matter.

This work is important because it challenges the normative identity itself—the destination, the goal: the belief that to be a real man means you get to believe that someone else is not as real. Through the work you do in counseling—and by the example of your own lives—you have an opportunity to create a revolutionary new sense of selfhood, one this world urgently needs: a sense of self that has the courage to will someone else's freedom.

About the Essays

Rapist Ethics

Adapted from a speech to first-year students at Hampshire College in Amherst, Massachusetts, September 8, 1978.

How Men Have (a) Sex

Adapted from a speech first delivered at Ohio State University, Columbus, Ohio, November 15, 1985, sponsored by the Office of Women's Services in conjunction with an art exhibit at the University Gallery titled "Rape." Also given at Haverford College, April 7, 1987 (sponsored by The Dialog About Men); Brown University, November 13, 1987 (sponsored by Collectively Changing Men and Brother-to-Brother); Carleton College, January 26, 1988 (sponsored by Student Movement Against Sexual Harassment [SMASH]); and Michigan State University, January 27, 1988 (sponsored by MSU Colloquium on Sexual Issues).

Refusing to Be a Man

Sexual Objectification and Male Supremacy

Based on a speech at Hampshire College in Amherst, Massachusetts, on February 12, 1980, sponsored by the Hampshire College Gay Men's Alliance. First published in *M.: Gentle Men for Gender Justice*, No. 5, Spring 1981; reprinted as "The Dirty Little Secret: Sexual Objectification and Male Supremacy" in *New York Native*, No. 38, May 24–June 6, 1982; copyright 1981, 1982 by John Stoltenberg.

Eroticism and Violence in the Father-Son Relationship

Adapted from a speech in Woodstock, New York, October 10, 1975 (co-sponsored by The Woodstock Women's Center and The Woodstock Self-Defense Committee) and at the Changing Men Conference, January 24, 1976, Burlington County College, Pemberton, New Jersey. First published in *For Men Against Sexism: A Book of Readings*, edited by Jon Snodgrass (Albion, California: Times Change Press, 1977); copyright 1976 by John Stoltenberg.

Disarmament and Masculinity

Adapted from a discussion guide written originally in 1975 to be distributed among supporters of a "Continental Walk" action, which was being organized across the United States by War Resisters League to call for disarmament and social justice. The WRL organizers rejected this manuscript, however, *Win* magazine (the pacifist weekly) rejected it, and it was not finally published until long after the walk—in 1978, by Susan Hester's Frog in the Well press. First published as "An Outline Guide and Bibliography for Studying the Connection Between Sexual Violence and War" (Palo Alto, California: Frog in the Well, 1978); copyright 1978 by John Stoltenberg.

The Fetus as Penis: Men's Self-interest and Abortion Rights

A speech at the Fifth National Conference on Men and Masculinity (the theme of which was "Men Overcoming Sexism") at the University of California,

About the Essays

Los Angeles, December 28, 1978. First published as "The Fetus as Penis: Male Self-interest and Abortion Rights" in *M.: Gentle Men for Gender Justice*, No. 3, Summer/Fall 1980; copyright 1980 by John Stoltenberg.

What Is "Good Sex"?

Expanded from a speech at the Gay Community Center in Philadelphia, Pennsylvania, January 15, 1983. First published as " 'Good Sex' and Gay Male Pornography" in *New York Native*, July 18-31, 1983; reprinted as "On Gay Male Pornography and 'Good Sex,' " in *M.: Gentle Men for Gender Justice*, No. 12, Spring-Summer 1984; copyright 1983, 1984 by John Stoltenberg.

The Forbidden Language of Sex

Adapted from remarks on a panel called "Eros, Language and Pornography" October 10, 1981, during the American Writers Congress at the Roosevelt Hotel in New York City.

Pornography and Freedom

Adapted from a speech delivered at a feminist conference on pornography at the University of Massachusetts, Amherst, April 28, 1984, where I dedicated it to the memory of antipornography activist Lynn Campbell; in Minneapolis, Minnesota, May 13, 1984, sponsored by the Pornography Resource Center, University Gay & Lesbian Community, United Ministries, Men Against Rape, and Minnesota Forum/West Bank Union; in Washington, D.C., July 1, 1984, at the Ninth National Conference on Men and Masculinity; in Providence, Rhode Island, October 20, 1984, sponsored by Brother-to-Brother; and in Atlanta, Georgia, March 16, 1985, sponsored by the Men's Experience. First published in *Changing Men* (formerly *M.: Gentle Men for Gender Justice*), No. 15, Spring 1985; copyright 1985 by John Stoltenberg.

Refusing to Be a Man

Confronting Pornography as a Civil-Rights Issue

Based on several speeches given in support of the Dworkin/MacKinnon Civil-Rights Antipornography Ordinance, including in Minneapolis, Minnesota, May 13, 1984, sponsored by the Pornography Resource Center (which was renamed Organizing Against Pornography in 1986), University Gay & Lesbian Community, United Ministries, Men Against Rape, and Minnesota Forum/West Bank Union; in New Haven, Connecticut, February 17, 1985, sponsored by the First Unitarian Universalist Society of New Haven; in Providence, Rhode Island, August 3, 1985, sponsored by Women Against Violence Against Women and Brother-to-Brother; and in Cambridge, Massachusetts, October 30, 1985, sponsored by the Women's Caucus of Harvard Divinity School.

Feminist Activism and Male Sexual Identity

An address to the 7th National Conference on Men and Masculinity at Tufts University, Medford, Massachusetts, June 16, 1981. First published in *M.: Gentle Men for Gender Justice*, No. 6, Fall 1981; also excerpted in *Sojourner*, August 1981, Vol. 6, No. 12; copyright 1981 by John Stoltenberg.

Other Men

A speech to the 8th National Conference on Men and Masculinity, August 14, 1983, at the University of Michigan, Ann Arbor, Michigan. First published in *M.: Gentle Men for Gender Justice*, No. 11, Winter 1983-84; reprinted in *New Men, New Minds*, Franklin Abbott, editor (Freedom, California: The Crossing Press, 1987); copyright 1983, 1986 by John Stoltenberg.

Battery and the Will to Freedom

Keynote address to The Northeast Conference on Counseling Male Abusers, sponsored by Brother-to-Brother, November 13, 1987, in Providence, Rhode Island.

About the Essays

Other Essays by the Author

"Refusing to Be a Man," in *For Men Against Sexism*, edited by Jon Snodgrass (Albion, California: Times Change Press, 1977).

"Toward Gender Justice," in *For Men Against Sexism*, edited by Jon Snodgrass (Albion, California: Times Change Press, 1977).

"Sadomasochism: Eroticized Violence, Eroticized Powerlessness," in *Against Sadomasochism: A Radical Feminist Analysis*, edited by Robin Ruth Linden, Darlene R. Pagano, Diana E. H. Russell, and Susan Leigh Star (Palo Alto, California: Frog in the Well, 1982).

"Gays and the Propornography Movement: Having the Hots for Sex Discrimination," in *Men Confronting Pornography*, edited by Michael S. Kimmel (New York: Crown Publishers, 1989).

Notes

Rapist Ethics

1. Aristotle, *Poetics*, in *Aristotle: On Man in the Universe*, Louise Robes Loomis, editor (Princeton, New Jersey: D. Van Nostrand Company, Inc., 1943), p. 435.

2. See Shere Hite's landmark studies, *The Hite Report on Male Sexuality* (New York: Alfred A. Knopf, 1981) and *Women and Love: A Cultural Revolution in Progress* (New York: Alfred A. Knopf, 1988).

3. Quoted in Diana E. H. Russell, *The Politics of Rape: The Victim's Perspective* (New York: Stein and Day, 1975), p. 99.

4. Benjamin Karpman, *The Sexual Offender and His Offenses* (New York: The Julian Press, Inc., 1954), p. 72.

5. Quoted in undated literature distributed by Boston Women Against Violence Against Women.

6. Russell, *Politics of Rape*, p. 48.

7. Russell, *Politics of Rape*, p. 48.

8. The Marquis de Sade, *Juliette*, translated by Austryn Wainhouse (New York: Grove Press, Inc., 1968), p. 140.

9. Quoted in Natalie Gittelson, *Dominus: A Woman Looks at Men's Lives* (New York: Farrar, Straus and Giroux, 1978), p. 79.

10. Russell, *Politics of Rape*, p. 75–76.

11. Gittelson, *Dominus*, p. 13.

How Men Have (a) Sex

1. My source for the foregoing information about so-called sex determinants in the human species is a series of interviews I conducted with the sexologist Dr. John Money in Baltimore, Maryland, in 1979 for an article I wrote called "The Multisex Theorem," which was published in a shortened version as "Future Genders" in *Omni* magazine, May 1980, pp. 67–73 ff.

2. Dworkin, Andrea. *Woman Hating* (New York: Dutton, 1974), p. 174.

3. Dworkin, *Woman Hating*, p. 183 (Italics in original).

Sexual Objectification and Male Supremacy

1. See, for instance, Glenn V. Ramsey's interviews with seventh- and eighth-grade boys in Peoria, Illinois, in 1939, cited in Alfred C. Kinsey, et al., *Sexual Behavior in the Human Male* (Philadelphia: W. B. Saunders Company, 1948), pp. 164–165.

2. It is considered "normal" for young boys to act out antipathy for that which is female. Boys who *do not* are perceived to be developing in a way that is potentially, and alarmingly, deviant. Gender-identity specialist Robert Stoller provides a sketch of the standard for how boys are *supposed* to disidentify with females when he discusses a program of treatment for boys who are deemed to be very feminine—perhaps, it is feared, pretranssexual. After several years of treatment, Stoller says approvingly, masculine traits begin to develop in such boys. They

start to value their penises (for instance, they now stand up to urinate where before they sat); they develop phobias; they physically attack females—dolls and girls, with pleasure more than anger the dominant affect; much more intrusive play appears, such as throwing balls and charging into their mothers and

Notes

other females; they play spontaneously for the first time using male dolls and masculine toys; in their drawings, instead of showing only beautiful women, masculine males appear; and stories of attacks with guns and swords, with violence, danger, and damage are now invented.

(Robert J. Stoller. *Sex and Gender, Vol. II: The Transsexual Experiment* [New York: Jason Aronson, 1975], p. 28.)

Eroticism and Violence in the Father-Son Relationship

1. Many of the values and insights in this essay are based on the theoretical work of Shulamith Firestone (*The Dialectic of Sex: The Case for Feminist Revolution,* [New York: Bantam, 1971]) and Andrea Dworkin (*Woman Hating,* [New York: Dutton, 1974]).

2. In the United States, this so-called marital-rape exclusion had been removed from the laws in only fourteen states by 1988. (Personal communication from Laurie Woods, director, National Center on Women and Family Law, New York City, January 22, 1988.)

3. Elizabeth Cady Stanton, "Address to the New York State Legislature, 1854," in *Feminism: The Essential Historical Writings,* Miriam Schneir, editor (New York: Vintage, 1972), pp. 110–116.

4. "Married Women's Property Act, New York, 1860," in Schneir, *Feminism,* pp. 122–124.

5. Juliet Mitchell, "On Freud and the Distinction Between the Sexes," in *Women and Analysis,* Jean Strouse, editor (New York: Grossman, 1974), pp. 27–36.

6. Stanton, in Schneir, *Feminism,* pp. 110–116.

7. See Phyllis Chesler, *Mothers on Trial: The Battle for Children and Custody* (New York: McGraw-Hill, 1986).

8. Alice S. Rossi, "Maternalism, Sexuality and the New Feminism," in *Contemporary Sexual Behavior: Critical Issues in the 1970s,* J. Zubin and J. Money, editors (Johns Hopkins University Press, 1973), pp. 145–171, quoted in Adrienne Rich, "The Theft of Childbirth," *The New York Review of Books,* XXII (October 2, 1975), pp. 25– 30.

Refusing to Be a Man

Disarmament and Masculinity

"Sons or fathers, poor men or rich men . . .": Phyllis Chesler, from *About Men* (New York: Simon and Schuster, 1978), p. 103.

"It should require no great imaginative leap . . .": Mary Daly, from "Transvaluation of Values: The End of Phallic Morality," chapter four of *Beyond God the Father* (Boston: Beacon Press, 1973), pp. 98–131.

"As a woman totally committed to the feminist cause . . .": Susan Brownmiller, from "War," chapter three of *Against Our Will: Men, Women and Rape* (New York: Simon and Schuster, 1975), pp. 31–113.

"Movement men are generally interested in women . . .": Marge Piercy, from "The Grand Coolie Damn," in *Sisterhood Is Powerful*, Robin Morgan, editor (New York: Vintage Books, 1970), pp. 421–438.

"Pornography is the theory, and rape the practice. . . .": Robin Morgan, from "Theory and Practice: Pornography and Rape," in *Going Too Far: The Personal Chronicle of a Feminist* (New York: Random House, 1977), pp. 163–169.

"[A]ny commitment to nonviolence which is real . . .": Andrea Dworkin, from "Redefining Nonviolence," in *Our Blood: Prophecies and Discourses on Sexual Politics* (New York: Harper & Row, 1976), pp. 66–72.

"White males are most responsible . . .": Robin Morgan, from "Goodbye to All That," in *Going Too Far: The Personal Chronicle of a Feminist* (New York: Random House, 1977), pp. 121–130.

"I can not say that I think you very generous . . .": Abigail Adams, from her letters in *The Feminist Papers: From Adams to de Beauvoir*, Alice S. Rossi, editor (New York: Bantam, 1973), p. 13.

"In the abolition movement . . .": Andrea Dworkin, from "Our Blood: The Slavery of Women in Amerika," in *Our Blood: Prophecies and Discourses on Sexual Politics* (New York: Harper & Row, 1976), pp. 76–95.

"To put it bluntly, . . .": Gary Mitchell Wandachild, "Complacency in the Face of Patriarchy," in *For Men Against Sexism: A Book of Readings*, Jon Snodgrass, editor (Albion, California: Times Change Press, 1977), pp. 83–97.

"Therefore if you insist . . .": Virginia Woolf, *Three Guineas* (New York: Harcourt, Brace & World, 1966.)

"Then Abraham lifted up the boy . . .": Søren Kierkegaard, "Prelude," in *Fear and Trembling*, translated by Walter Lowrie (Garden City, New York: Doubleday & Company, Inc., 1954), pp. 26–29.

Notes

"Georg shrank into a corner . . .": Franz Kafka, "The Judgment," in *The Penal Colony*, translated by Willa and Edwin Muir (New York: Schocken Books, 1963), pp. 49–63.

"It is also true . . .": Franz Kafka, *Letter to His Father*, translated by Ernst Kaiser and Eithne Wilkins (New York: Schocken Books, 1966).

"*[T]he only way that the Oedipus Complex* . . .": Shulamith Firestone, "Freudianism: The Misguided Feminism," chapter three of *The Dialectic of Sex* (New York: Bantam Books, 1970), pp. 41–71.

"In war, the fathers castrate the sons . . .": Andrea Dworkin, "Why So-called Radical Men Love and Need Pornography," in *Take Back the Night: Women on Pornography*, Laura Lederer, editor (New York: William Morrow and Company, Inc., 1980), pp. 148–154.

"Each man, knowing his own deep-rooted impulse . . .": Andrea Dworkin, from "The Root Cause," in *Our Blood: Prophecies and Discourses on Sexual Politics* (New York: Harper & Row, 1976), pp. 96–111.

"Nothing is more political to a feminist . . .": Andrea Dworkin, from "Marx and Gandhi Were Liberals—Feminism and the 'Radical' Left," pamphlet (Frog in the Well, P.O. Box 170052, San Francisco, California 94117, 1973).

"As the formula of 'fucking as conquest' . . .": Kate Millett, from "Norman Mailer," chapter seven of *Sexual Politics* (New York: Avon Books, 1970), pp. 314–335.

The Fetus as Penis: Men's Self-interest and Abortion Rights

1. National Center for Health Statistics, Department of Health, Education, and Welfare, "Wanted and Unwanted Births Reported by Mothers 15–44 Years of Age: United States, 1973," *Advance Data from Vital and Health Statistics*, No. 9, August 10, 1977.

2. Jacqueline Darroch Forrest, Christopher Tietze, and Ellen Sullivan, "Abortion in the United States, 1976–1977," *Family Planning Perspectives*, 10: 271–279, September/October 1978.

3. On June 30, 1980, the Supreme Court ruled that the federal government and states were under no constitutional obligation to provide Medicaid funding for abortions; by 1981, Congress had cut off all Medicaid funds for all abortions except those needed to prevent a woman's death.

---

4. Forrest, "Abortion in the United States."

5. Linda Murray, "Searching for Safe Contraceptives," *Contemporary Ob/Gyn*, 9: 37–54, May 1977; "Population Research Funding Declines," *Planned Parenthood-World Population Washington Memo*, December 15, 1978, p. 4.

6. Dr. Christopher Tietze, director of abortion research activities for The Population Council, New York City, personal communication, December 6, 1978, based on figures for 1976.

7. Centers for Disease Control, Department of Health, Education, and Welfare, *Abortion Surveillance 1976*, issued August 1978.

8. Forrest, "Abortion in the United States." The Supreme Court has so far let stand lower court decisions allowing both public and private hospitals to refuse to perform abortions at all; as a result, clinics and private physicians have become the primary providers of abortion services.

9. William H. Spillane and Paul E. Ryser, "Male Household Heads' Attitudes Concerning Contraception, Abortion, and Related Policy Issues, Pittsburgh 1971," (unpublished report, Population Division, Graduate School of Public Health, University of Pittsburgh), pp. 109–110.

10. "Chicago: 'Outreach' Is the Name of the Game," *The Family Planner*, 8: 2–4, March/April 1977.

11. "Chicago: 'Outreach.' "

12. *11 Million Teenagers: What Can Be Done About the Epidemic of Adolescent Pregnancies in the United States* (New York: The Alan Guttmacher Institute, 1976).

13. Maria C. Boria-Berna, "Husband's Role in Birth Control Acceptance," *Medical Aspects of Human Sexuality*, 5: 70–74, May 1972.

14. Aeschylus, *The Eumenides*, lines 658–661, in *Oresteia*, translated by Richard Lattimore (Chicago: The University of Chicago Press, 1953), p. 158.

15. Sigmund Freud, "Femininity," in *New Introductory Lectures on Psychoanalysis*, translated and edited by James Strachey (New York: W. W. Norton & Company, Inc., 1965), p. 128.

16. Andrea Dworkin, "The Sexual Politics of Fear and Courage," in *Our Blood: Prophecies and Discourses on Sexual Politics* (New York: Harper & Row, 1976), p. 55.

17. Michael B. Bracken et al., "Abortion Counseling: An Experimental Study of Three Techniques," *American Journal of Obstetrics and Gynecology*, 117: 10–20, September 1, 1973.

Notes

18. Mary E. Swigar et al., "Interview Follow-up of Abortion Applicant Dropouts," *Social Psychiatry*, 11: 135–143, July 15, 1976.
19. Ellen W. Freeman, "Abortion: Subjective Attitudes and Feelings," *Family Planning Perspectives*, 10: 150–155, May/June 1978.
20. Bracken, "Abortion Counseling."
21. Arden Aibel Rothstein, "Men's Reactions to Their Partners' Elective Abortions," *American Journal of Obstetrics and Gynecology*, 128: 831–837, August 15, 1977.

The Forbidden Language of Sex

1. Susan Duncan, *The Lewd Stepfather* (P.O. Box 486, South Laguna, California 92677: Publisher's Consultants, 1978), p. 142.
2. Samuel Mixer, *Bondage Fling* (Los Angeles: Sutton House Publishing Co., Inc., 1977), p. 103.
3. *Slave Girls: Whipped, Tied & Trained* (New York: Star Distributors, Ltd., 1978), pp. 119–120.
4. Henry Miller, *Sexus* (New York: Grove Press, 1965), p. 384; quoted in *Sexual Politics* by Kate Millett (New York: Avon Books, 1971), p. 306.

Pornography and Freedom

1. Edward Baker, *Tricked Into White Slavery* (P.O. Box 486, South Laguna, California 92677: Publisher's Consultants, 1978), p. 132.
2. *The Shamed Beauty* (P.O. Box 362 Canal Street Station, New York, New York 10013: Star Distributors, Ltd.), p. 60.
3. Eli Robeson, "Knife Point," *Folsom Magazine*, No. 2 [1981?], p. 27.

Confronting Pornography as a Civil-Rights Issue

1. Robin Morgan. "Women Disrupt the Miss America Pageant," *Going Too Far: The Personal Chronicle of a Feminist* (New York: Random House, 1977), pp. 62–67.

2. Chicago *Seed*, July 30, 1971, quoted in Robin Lake, "The Playboy & Miss America Protests: First Targets of Feminist Revolt," *Newspage* (published by Women Against Violence in Pornography and Media), Vol. 3, No. 8.

3. Susan Braudy, "The Article I Wrote on Women That *Playboy* Wouldn't Publish," *Glamour*, May 1971, p. 202, quoted in Lake, "Playboy & Miss America Protests."

4. Robin Morgan, "On Violence and Feminist Basic Training," *Going Too Far*, pp. 132–133.

5. "Really Socking It to Women," *Time*, February 7, 1977.

6. See, for instance, *Take Back the Night: Women on Pornography*, edited by Laura Lederer (New York: Morrow, 1980); and *Pornography: Men Possessing Women*, by Andrea Dworkin (New York: Perigee, 1981).

7. See, for instance, *Pornography and Sexual Aggression*, edited by Neil M. Malamuth and Edward Donnerstein (New York: Academic Press, 1984), and *Connections Between Sex and Aggression*, by Dolf Zillman (Hillsdale, New Jersey: Lawrence Erlbaum Associates, Publishers, 1984).

8. *Ordeal*, by Linda Lovelace with Mike McGrady (Secaucus, New Jersey: Citadel Press, 1980).

9. See *Out of Bondage*, by Linda Lovelace with Mike McGrady (New York: Citadel Press, 1986).

10. See Catharine A. MacKinnon, *Sexual Harassment of Working Women* (New Haven: Yale, 1979).

11. See Andrea Dworkin, *Woman Hating* (New York: Dutton, 1974), pp. 51–90.

12. Reprinted in Andrea Dworkin, *Letters from a War Zone* (London: Secker & Warburg, 1988).

13. See Andrea Dworkin, *Pornography: Men Possessing Women* (New York: Perigee, 1981), and *Right-wing Women* (New York: Perigee, 1983).

14. Andrea Dworkin, unpublished testimony, Zoning and Planning Committee, City of Minneapolis, October 18, 1983 (on file at Organizing Against Pornography, 734 East Lake Street, Minneapolis, Minnesota 55407).

15. Catharine A. MacKinnon, unpublished testimony, Zoning and Planning Committee, City of Minneapolis, October 18, 1983 (on file at Organizing Against Pornography).

16. Dworkin, October 18, 1983, testimony.

Notes

17. Undated press release, December 1983 (on file at Organizing Against Pornography).

18. "Minneapolis Asked to Attack Pornography as Rights Issue," *The New York Times*, December 18, 1983; Jeanne Barkey, "Feminists Pioneer Civil Rights Legislation," *Minneapolis Citizens Against Pornography*, Vol. 1, No. 1, Summer 1984 (newsletter on file at Organizing Against Pornography).

19. *Public Hearings on Ordinances to Add Pornography as Discrimination Against Women*, Minneapolis City Council, Government Operations Committee (edition published by Organizing Against Pornography), p. 14.

20. *Public Hearings*, p. 15.

21. *Public Hearings*, p. 16.

22. "Model Antipornography Civil-Rights Ordinance," in *Pornography and Civil Rights: A New Day for Women's Equality*, by Andrea Dworkin and Catharine A. MacKinnon (Minneapolis, Minnesota: Organizing Against Pornography, 1988), pp. 139–140.

23. Research conducted by Diana E. H. Russell, reported in her book *Rape in Marriage* (New York: Macmillan, 1982), pp. 83–84.

24. Excerpts from Diana E. H. Russell's research cited by Dr. Pauline Bart in her testimony before the Minneapolis City Council December 12, 1983, *Public Hearings*, pp. 19–20.

25. "Model Antipornography Civil–Rights Ordinance," in Dworkin and MacKinnon, *Pornography and Civil Rights*, p. 138.

26. From *Men on Rape*, by Timothy Beneke (New York: St. Martin's Press, 1982), pp. 71–74.

27. "An Ordinance of the City of Minneapolis," in Dworkin and MacKinnon, *Pornography and Civil Rights*, p. 101.

28. "Code of Indianapolis and Marion County Indiana," in Dworkin and MacKinnon, *Pornography and Civil Rights*, pp. 113–114.

29. Paraphrased from "Pornography Is a Civil Rights Issue," the testimony of Andrea Dworkin before the Attorney General's Commission on Pornography, January 22, 1986, in *Letters From a War Zone*, by Andrea Dworkin (London: Secker & Warburg, 1988), pp. 285–286.

30. Only 7.8 percent of women never encounter sexual harassment or assault in their lifetime, as calculated by Diana E. H. Russell from her data, cited in Catharine A. MacKinnon, "Pornography, Civil Rights, and Speech," *Harvard*

Civil Rights-Civil Liberties Review, Vol. 20, No. 1, winter 1985 (footnote 31).

31. Dworkin, "Pornography Is a Civil-Rights Issue," p. 286.

32. "Appendix to Jurisdictional Statement" for appeal to the United States Supreme Court, October term, 1985, in *Hudnut, et al. vs. American Booksellers Association, et al.*, filed by Mark Dall and Kathryn A. Watson for the City of Indianapolis, p. B–22.

33. For instance, *Roberts v. U.S. Jaycees* (1984), in which the Supreme Court said the government's purpose to eliminate sex discrimination raises "compelling state interests" that can outweigh First Amendment rights to freedom of association.

34. "Appendix," p. B–35.

35. *The New York Times*, July 11, 1985, p. 22.

36. Decision by Frank Esterbrook reprinted in "Appendix to Jurisdictional Statement," pp. A–11, A–12.

37. "Jurisdictional Statement" for appeal to the United States Supreme Court, October term, 1985, in *Hudnut, et al. vs. American Booksellers Association, et al.*, filed by Mark Dall and Kathryn A. Watson for the City of Indianapolis, pp. 10–11.

38. "Appendix to Jurisdictional Statement."

39. Theresa Monsour, "Pornography Law Author Blasts Ruling," (St. Paul) *Pioneer Press Dispatch*, February 25, 1986.

40. Susan Sherman Fadem, "Court Throws Out Anti-Porn Law," *St. Louis Globe Democrat*, February 25, 1986.

41. In her testimony before the Attorney General's Commission January 22, 1986.

Other Men

1. Andrea Dworkin, from "The Root Cause" in *Our Blood: Prophecies and Discourses on Sexual Politics* (New York: Perigee, 1981), pp. 109–110.

Notes

Selected Bibliography: The Civil-Rights Antipornography Ordinance

(See "Confronting Pornography as a Civil-Rights Issue," pp. 137–171.)

(Many of these items are available from Organizing Against Pornography, 734 East Lake Street, Minneapolis, Minnesota 55407.)

Baldwin, Margaret. "The Sexuality of Inequality: The Minneapolis Pornography Ordinance," *Law & Inequality: A Journal of Theory and Practice* (Vol. II, No. 2, August 1984, pp. 629–653). Summarizes the factual basis and legal theory underlying the Minneapolis City Council's finding that pornography "is central in creating and maintaining the civil inequality of the sexes" and is a "systematic practice of exploitation and subordination based on sex which differentially harms women." Quotes extensively from victims who testified during Minneapolis City Council's public hearings on the Ordinance. ("For those who do not understand either the outrage or the seriousness of women's struggle against pornography, the evidence of the harm attributable to pornography may clarify what is at stake for women. . . . That a man's orgasms are considered more valuable in this society than a woman's life is a simple and true indication both of how entrenched women's subordinate status is, and how subordinate it is.") Explains why obscenity law is legally inadequate as a remedy for the sex-based injuries fostered by pornography. Discusses remedies afforded by the Ordinance.

Brest, Paul, and Ann Vandenberg. "Politics, Feminism, and the Constitution: The Anti-Pornography Movement in Minneapolis," *Stanford Law Review* (Vol. 39, No. 3, February 1987). Essay and reportage on the history of the Civil-Rights Antipornography Ordinance in Minneapolis—including background on zoning ordinances, Dworkin and MacKinnon's legal theory, the public hearings they conducted, local press reaction, the City Council's votes to pass the Ordinance, and the mayor's vetoes. ("[F]or many citizens, participation in the campaign for the ordinance was the beginning of taking responsibility, and forcing their communities to take responsibility, for the images of pornography. Even those who had doubts about the ordinance were moved to see and acknowledge the misogynism of much pornography. Many women and men were profoundly affected by the anti-pornography campaigns—'transformed' would not be too strong. For Catharine MacKinnon, Andrea Dworkin, and their co-workers to have affected the consciousness of so many people was no small achievement.")

"Brief Amici Curiae of Women Against Pornography, et al." in the case of *William H. Hudnut, III, Mayor of the City of Indianapolis, Indiana, et al. vs. American Booksellers Association, Inc., et al.*, United States Court of Appeals for the Seventh Circuit, filed by Ralph A. Hummel, attorney for amici curiae. Argues that past efforts to curb pornography's harms have not succeeded but that the Ordinance would help victims of pornography and should be available.

Dworkin, Andrea. "Against the Male Flood: Censorship, Pornography, and Equality," *Harvard Women's Law Journal* (Vol. 8, Spring 1985). Analysis of censorship and legal obscenity and their relationship to writing. Discussion of difference between obscenity and pornography ("One reason that stopping pornographers and pornography is not censorship is that pornographers are more like the police in police states than they are like the writers in police states. They are the instruments of terror, not its victims. What police do to the powerless in police states is what pornographers do to women. . . ."). Discussion of social subordination and how in pornography it silences women. Discussion of legal impact on women's equality of civil-rights antipornography law. ("Pornography is inequality. The civil rights law would allow women to advance equality by removing the concrete discrimination and hurting economically those who make, sell, distribute, or exhibit it. . . . After [pornography] hurts [women] by being what it is and doing what it does, the civil rights law would allow us to hurt it back.") Contains appendix: "Model Anti-Pornography Law" as drafted by Dworkin and MacKinnon.

Dworkin, Andrea. "Brief Amicus Curiae of Andrea Dworkin" in the case of *William H. Hudnut, III, Mayor of the City of Indianapolis, Indiana, et al. vs. American Booksellers Association, Inc., et al.*, United States Court of Appeals for the Seventh Circuit. Argues that pornographers' rights of expression are outweighed by women's rights to equality.

Dworkin, Andrea. "Pornography Is a Civil Rights Issue," testimony before the Attorney General's Commission on Pornography in New York City January 22, 1986, *University of Michigan Journal of Law Reform*, Vol. 20: 3, 1988; reprinted in Andrea Dworkin, *Letters from a War Zone* (London, England: Secker & Warburg, 1988).

Dworkin, Andrea, and Catharine A. MacKinnon, *The Reasons Why: Essays on the New Civil Rights Law Recognizing Pornography as Sex Discrimination* (reprint

Notes

of Dworkin's "Against the Male Flood . . ." and MacKinnon's "Feminism, Pornography, and Law").

Dworkin, Andrea, and Catharine A. MacKinnon, *Pornography and Civil Rights: A New Day for Women's Equality* (Minneapolis, Minnesota: Organizing Against Pornography, 1988). Their most comprehensive presentation of the political theory and legal operation of the Ordinance they coauthored.

Gershel, Michael A. "Evaluating a Proposed Civil Rights Approach to Pornography: Legal Analysis As If Women Mattered," *William Mitchell Law Review* (Vol. 11, 1985, pp. 41–80). Addresses the constitutionality of the Ordinance in the light of current First Amendment doctrine and argues for the legality of a new exception to protected speech, an exception based on the concept of pornography as a violation of women's civil rights.

Hoffman, Eric. "Feminism, Pornography, and Law," *University of Pennsylvania Law Review*, Vol. 133: 497–534, 1985. Discusses the Ordinance in terms of feasibility and political strategy. ("The strength of legislatively designed tort actions, such as the Minneapolis Ordinance, lies in their form as amendments to municipal civil rights laws. . . . The state role is confined to adjudication, and the factual presentation of the cases is left to those who claim to be harmed. This allows feminist plaintiffs to exercise some control over the development of claims under the statutes.")

Hoyt, Charlee. "Pornography and Women's Civil Rights," *Response*, Fall 1984, pp. 5–7. Summary of the Ordinance by one of its cosponsors on the Minneapolis City Council.

"Jurisdictional Statement" for appeal to the United States Supreme Court, October term, 1985, from the Seventh Circuit Court of Appeals in the case of *William H. Hudnut, III, Mayor of the City of Indianapolis, Indiana, et al. vs. American Booksellers Association, Inc., et al.*, filed by Mark Dall and Kathryn A. Watson, attorneys for the City of Indianapolis.

MacKinnon, Catharine A. "On Collaboration," her speech at the sixteenth National Women and Law Conference, in Catharine A. MacKinnon, *Feminism Unmodified* (Cambridge, Massachusetts: Harvard University Press, 1987), pp. 198–205. Argues against so-called feminist opposition to the Ordinance.

MacKinnon, Catharine A. "Not a Moral Issue," *Yale Law & Policy Review* (Vol. II, No. 2, Spring 1984, pp. 321–345); reprinted in Catharine A. MacKinnon, *Feminism Unmodified* (Cambridge, Massachusetts: Harvard University Press, 1987), pp. 146–162. Analysis of difference between obscenity and pornography

("Obscenity law is concerned with morality, specifically morals from the male point of view, meaning the standpoint of male dominance. The feminist critique of pornography is a politics, specifically politics from women's point of view, meaning the standpoint of the subordination of women to men. Morality here means good and evil; politics means power and powerlessness. Obscenity is a moral idea; pornography is concrete. . . . Obscenity as such probably does little harm; pornography causes attitudes and behaviors of violence and discrimination which define the treatment and status of half the population"). Discussion of how obscenity law—by seeming to put state power behind a prohibition of what men can have access to—actually protects both the sexiness of pornography and the availability of it.

MacKinnon, Catharine A. "Pornography, Civil Rights, and Speech," *Harvard Civil Rights-Civil Liberties Law Review*, Vol. 20, No. 1, Winter 1985; reprinted in Catharine A. MacKinnon *Feminism Unmodified* (Cambridge, Massachusetts: Harvard University Press, 1987), pp. 163–197. Discussion of pornography as a practice of sex discrimination ("What pornography *does* goes beyond its content: It eroticizes hierarchy, it sexualizes inequality. . . . [Pornography] institutionalizes the sexuality of male supremacy, fusing the eroticization of dominance and submission with the social construction of male and female"). Explanation of the legal theory behind defining pornography as a practice of sex discrimination and the four injuries that the Ordinance makes actionable: coercion into pornography, forcing pornography on a person, assault caused by pornography, trafficking in pornography.

Memo to Minneapolis City Council from Catharine A. MacKinnon and Andrea Dworkin, December 26, 1983, unpublished, on file at Organizing Against Pornography.

"Note" (unsigned editorial comment), *Harvard Law Review* (Vol. 98, No. 460, December 1984, pp. 460–481). Examines whether full First Amendment protection should be given to pornography as feminists have defined it—sexually explicit pictures or words that associate women's physical abuse or degradation with sexual pleasure. Examines existing exceptions to First Amendment protection—incitement to illegal acts, obscenity, group libel—and finds justification for according pornography a similarly disfavored constitutional status.

"Public Hearings on Ordinances to Add Pornography as Discrimination Against Women," Minneapolis City Council, Government Operations Committee, December 12 and 13, 1983.

Notes

Stanton, Therese. "Fighting for Our Existence," *Changing Men*, No. 15, Fall 1985, pp. 21–22. Essay on neighborhood activism and victim testimony, by a community organizer for the Ordinance.

White, Van F. "Pornography and Pride," *Changing Men*, No. 15, Fall 1985, pp. 17–18. Essay on relation between pornography and racism, by a cosponsor of the Minneapolis Civil-Rights Antipornography Ordinance. Originally published in *Essence* magazine, September 1984.

M

M

I